C0-DAL-017

ROADSONGS

A Journey into the Life and Mindscapes of an American Artist

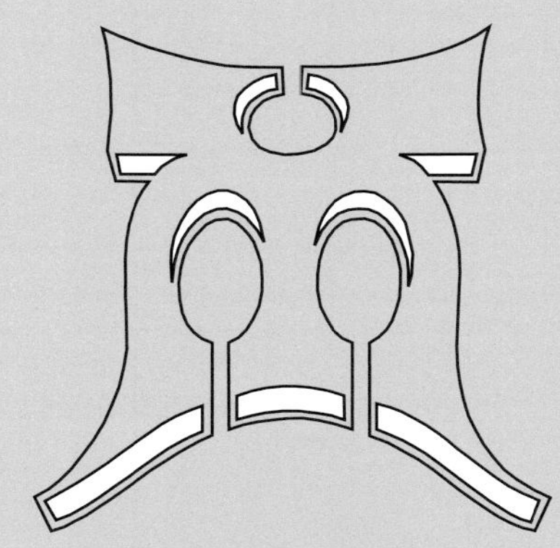

Malcolm Graeme Childers

Edited by Pamela Barnard Childers

FOR MY FRIEND GEORGE WILLIAMS III
In the Premier Edition,
PROOF this book is
number AP#1 of 3000 examples.
WITH GREAT RESPECT FOR HIS INSPIRATION IN THE AUDIO CONCEPT OF THE SIERRA AUDIO PIECE MALCOLM GRAEME CHILDERS

A Joint Publication of
The Real Earth and Wind River Productions, Incorporated
Chattanooga, Tennessee

MMI

ROADSONGS: A Journey into the Life and Mindscapes of an American Artist

For information, visit our website at
http://www.roadsongs.com
phone The Real Earth at 1-888-488-6714,
or write Wind River Productions, Inc.,
820 Scenic Highway, Lookout Mountain, Tennessee 37350

Library of Congress Control Number : 00-090495
ISBN: 0-9672-612-0-1
Graphic Design by Malcolm Graeme Childers, Walden, TN

Printed in the United States by
Jones Printing Company, Chattanooga, TN,
a division of Master Graphics, Memphis, TN.
Jointly Published by The Real Earth and
Wind River Productions, Incorporated.

Table of Contents

Dedication

This book is dedicated to my hope that those virtues in the human spirit, which move us to revere this planet and to live in harmony with each other and all the forms of life found here, will quickly replace our endemic darker inclinations. Since any future goodness that we can influence will come from thoughts and actions that produce the highest quality of life for the greatest diversity of life forms on this Earth, my hope is borne of a gravity far deeper than mere wishful thinking. My hope is no less than a primal desire to see our conscious species live on in the rich multitude of other living things we are just beginning to comprehend. Without the fruition of such hopes, neither this body of work nor any other art will matter,

nor will we.

Acknowledgments

First, I will be forever grateful to my wife Pamela Barnard Childers for her editorial effort, faith, love, and earnest support in the creation of this book. Without her, this book would likely have remained only a dream. My sincere thanks to Mark Caldwell for his timely business counsel, long-term support of my artistic work, and his tireless participation in this project. To the following individuals who have at some point had an influence on this book, I wish to express my sincere appreciation: Jim Bolling for his marketing studies; Jon Franz, Daniel and Kathryn Westcott, Ray Wong, Dennis DeHainaut, and Erin Kilpatrick for their graphic expertise; Stephen Bigger and Dan Landrum for arranging and producing the road music; Stephen Wells for producing and recording "Out on the Highway"; May Wood for her acting; John Hagan for his '53 Chevy pickup and cutting torch sounds; T. W. Francescon and kin for their sounds of youth and family; manuscript reviewers Tanya Cadd, John Rogers, Jerry Sorrels, Tom Cory, Roy and Jenny Smith, Joel A. Barker, John Wright, Lanny and Barbara Mauldin, Julia and E.B. West, Carla McDonough, David and Ginnie Harris, Ruth and Loren Book, and George Barnard. I also thank those who have gone out of their way to help this stranger with his questions and requests, like the biker who started up his chopper outside of the Lost Hog Bar in Oro Grande and took off twice just so I could get a good audio take, the engineer who helped me record locomotives in Gallup, New Mexico, or the team of geologists from New Mexico State University who pulled my van out of sand near a dry lake bed in Utah.

In a less direct but equal way, I wish to acknowledge the following influences: visualists Leonardo Da Vinci, William Blake, John Constable, J.M.W. Turner, Holman Hunt, Vincent Van Gogh, Georges Seurat, Elihu Vedder, Fredrick Edwin Church, Thomas Moran, M.C. Escher, Yoshida Hiroshi, Charles Sheeler, Thomas Hart Benton, and Gene Franks; writers Edgar Lee Masters, John Muir, John Steinbeck, Edward Abbey, Barry Lopez, John Mc Phee, Wendell Berry, William Least Heat Moon, and Craig Crist-Evans; media arts producers Garrison Keillor, James Burke, Richard Attenborough, Ken Burns, Bill Moyers, Ken Nordeen, and the creators of National Public Radio's news magazines; composer/musicians Turlough O' Carolan, Ralph Vaughan Williams, Aaron Copeland, Virgil Thomson, Ian Tyson, Gordon Lightfoot, Jackson Browne, and Philip Aaberg.

By Way of Explanation

This book originated from my desire to explore the avenues of aesthetic communication between myself and the varied imaginations of my audience. In order to remain consistent with the spirit of that exploration, I have chosen to let the imagery, the poetic and concurrent texts (literary and spoken), the audio landscapes, and the musical passages develop toward their natural conclusions free of any pre-existing definitions or paradigms.

Given such a mandate, any similarity between the art expressions found herein and established formal paradigms of art, literature, or music would tend to be purely coincidental.

Since my work tends more toward expressionism than formalism, I make no apology for these "form" anomalies. There are many instances of paradigm-free creative solutions in this book, but the design of some texts may be the most obvious.

Narrow Column Prose:

I found columns more suitable for most of the art texts. As in poetry, line breaks tend to inform the reader about the rhythm, phrasing and, in turn, the spirit of what is written.

Speaker Specific Text:

In writing passages that are heavy with dialogue, I found the constant need to identify respective speakers tedious. In some of the drama-oriented texts, I have addressed the "He said-She said" problem by specific speaker column placement on the page. For example, in the text to "The Semi" (pages 28, 30-32), there are four voices: the narrator, Gandy, Beuf and the waitress. By giving each character his own column, I have diminished the need to identify who is talking. This frees the text to deal with attitudes and descriptive body language. As I was working out the "how" of *speaker specific text,* another expressive idea occurred to me.

Character-Oriented Fonts:

It occurred to me, as I was looking through my font options, that there is a strong coincidence between the way we speak as individuals and the way some fonts appear in text. Few of us ever speak with the clear diction of good actors. Personal style, upbringing, regional or ethnic accents, and genetic predispositions form the reality of both our speech patterns and common experience. Since this is the case, how do you create within a column of words (beyond any specific pronunciation) the visual effect of listening to someone who mumbles so much that he or she is hard to understand?

The color of rich ethnic or regional accents can be lost in a uniform text font. I feel that some fonts (even when they are hard to read) provide a plausible additional avenue of expression.

Looking Down a Road of Songs

Introduction

I must have just turned seven. Now some forty-eight years later, I am surprised at the clarity of my mental images from that age. I am sure that some details have been altered by our common propensity to create a personal myth. I wish I could separate fact from fancy, but unfortunately such losses are integral to the nature of human memory. So, for whatever value there is in contemplating myths, these were mine.

As a young man, my father weathered the privations of the 1929 Depression. That arduous experience left him with a compulsive romance for security and affluence, which has become the fingerprint of so many people who have been forced to endure hard times.

Somewhere in the pinch of thin shoes and empty pockets, he must have promised himself that if chance ever smiled his way, he would buy the most elegant automobile he could afford.

One late spring morning, my older sister Tanya, my younger sister Dagmar, and I were playing house on the front porch. We had stretched old blankets across the railings and fastened them with our mother's clothespins, making a motley tent with rooms.

Having just reached architectural satisfaction with our early bedroom-revival hacienda, I was thinking about kicking back with a tall glass of lemonade. Tanya was fixing a small hole in the roof when she happened to glance out of our little triangular window.

"Holy Cow! Look at this neat car!" she said, gesturing with a clothespin. Down Idaho Avenue, past the Fords, Chevys, DeSotos, and Mercurys came a magnificent 1939 V-12 Packard limousine. Our curiosity really piqued when the American dream car pulled up in front of our government project home. It became total amazement when the driver's door opened, and our father got out.

Chance had smiled. He had finessed a deal with an elderly lady who lived in a large white house hidden in the sea of orange groves that surrounded Riverside, California, in those days. Apparently the lady was getting up in years and the big car, which had been kept in a garage since it was new, finally became too difficult for her to handle. So with some regret and probably equal relief, Mrs. Snow passed it on for a mere $1400.

We scrambled out from under the blankets and down the steps toward the street. "Is this our car?" Dagmar asked, her eyes alive with excitement, as my dad came up the sidewalk.

Wow! My distorted reflection in the polished indigo paint seemed to come from deep within the metal. Each long, sweeping front fender was adorned with an encased spare tire and topped off with a chrome rearview mirror. The wide whitewall tires and pinstriped wheels had chrome moon hubcaps, each bearing Packard's distinct red hexagon insignia.

This limousine would eventually become a classic, and rightly so, for it was a prime example of cosmopolitan prestige during the last years of the Depression. It was, most likely, one of the last great American touring cars. The cast iron luggage rack over the rear bumper was there so that the well-heeled traveler could strap down steamer trunks, neatly packed with chic wardrobes, to be chauffeured from one scenic grand hotel to the next, no doubt passing families devastated by dust and depression along the way.

Later, when my sisters and I got to take day trips in the limousine, we would beg to ride on the luggage rack when we were on back roads. We, in our childlike innocence, surmised that Mr. Packard really knew how to please kids and had put this special thing back there just for us.

My father's struggle to make ends meet, while he owned the Packard, belied his devotion to the hope of grandness that the American Dream offered before the market for distinctive craftsmanship began to fade in those difficult years before the Second World War. I would not have understood the subtle ironies in my parents' values back then. Ironies have a curious way of appearing more substantial in a rearview mirror.

One of the most influential gifts they gave me as a child was our financially lean family *biting the bullet* and taking one long trip in the Packard limousine. It was our first and only RV. To cut trip expenses, my parents often made their bed on the luxurious carpet that covered the extended floor in the passenger area. My sisters and I would sleep on the seats.

One evening in the glow of twilight, my dad pulled off Highway 89 near Cottonwood, Arizona, and eased down a gravel road to the banks of the Verde River. I was limp and groggy when my mother laid me in the front seat, and within a few minutes, I was fast asleep.

The morning sun, peeking over a high river bench on the far bank, brought me back into a land more magical than many of my dreams. Reaching high over the car in the warm morning light were the limbs of great cottonwoods.

I hunched up quietly to avoid waking anyone. Carefully pushing the chrome handle down while pulling on the arm rest, I got the door to open. I slipped out and gently closed it behind me. Turning around, I faced a delicately lit vista of wildness and grace.

The cottonwoods, their great grey trunks anchored deep through a carpet of thick short grass, arched almost halfway over the river bed. I heard the breeze first in the dance of leaves, then felt its cool touch on my face.

Turning slightly, I could just make out seven mustangs, obscured by willows in a back eddy on the far bank. Entranced by the primeval beauty of the moment, I watched them drink cautiously among the river stones. Just then the back door opened behind me with a loud clunk, and my dad stumbled out, yawning and scratching.

The mustang herd bolted in a spray of water, back through the willow thicket and up the dusty bench into the rising sun. I watched bright dust drift from the place where they had disappeared over the rim. Then, I was surprised to see the stallion return. He looked down from the bench and whinnied stridently, as if he were castigating me for catching him with his tongue down. I was snickering to myself as he vanished back over the rim when, all of a sudden, my dad grabbed me from behind and scolded me for standing on sand, in socks soaking wet with the morning dew.

Though it was just a fleeting moment, it was magic. It has long remained vivid in my memory because in that moment I first began to value the sanity and freedom of wild things.

The great old car did its work well, purring powerfully down any western highway my old man chose to aim that six-foot hood. It was a time when the road was made personal by the individuality of towns that you had to go through, before America gradually became homogenized by generous infusions of freeways and television.

My old man sat in the driver's seat of absolute authority, handing out edicts, admonitions and sentences to my sisters and me in the coach class seats. My mother, the peacemaker/ navigator, spent much of her time greasing the wheels of daily progress with diplomacy and kindness.

Indio, Yuma, Phoenix, Jerome, Cottonwood, Sedona, Flagstaff, Petrified Forest, Painted Desert, Grand Canyon, Marble Canyon, Vermilion Cliffs, Zion, Las Vegas, Reno, Portland--then northwest to an island in the Columbia River, and then south all the way back down the miles of forested coast through Oregon, and California; we saw the land.

My sisters and I would squabble off and on, my parents continually threatened never to take us anywhere else again, but most of the time I would be looking out the window as long as I could keep my eyes open. Humming quietly to myself, I would make up musical tunes as I stared at the great American West rushing by outside.

Somewhere on this journey, I sensed that the landscape had an emotional impact on me. At times the experience seemed very private--like being in an envelope of concentration, focused on the mystical effect that sun or moonlight had on clouds, great expansive plains, buttes, and mountain faces.

In a strange and wonderful way, all of this added up to music in my young mind. I would quietly hum to myself the melodies that I felt, but in my mind I heard the power of great string orchestras. The delicate transparency of oboe, English horn, harp, or solo violin carried counter melodies and phrases high over bass violins into transcending passages, as the landscape gradually changed on the other side of my window on the wild.

These were my first road songs.

The Packard eventually found the same place in my father's experience that it had in the mind of its previous owner. The V-12 engine got only eight miles per gallon, and gas was no longer twenty cents. He tied a tarpaulin over the roof to keep rainwater from leaking into the white canvas top, cursing the stupidity of such engineering traditions. After a few years, the engine froze up from disuse. Then one day, he just got tired of his old dreams and sold what was left of that one to a deaf mechanic for a hundred and fifty dollars.

Occasionally I have wondered how different things might have been if he had just started the engine once a week, sealed the roof with sheet metal, blocked it up so that the tires were off the ground, and tarped it more diligently. He might have been able to sell it as a running classic for enough to retire early instead of having to work the swing shift all those extra years. I know such thoughts are decades too late to affect the flow of choice and chance.

Still, something remains of my father's desire to experience grandness; something has survived the years and his many errors of judgment.

I have not forgotten my road songs.

These I pass on to anyone who is willing to look long enough at this infinitely virtuous Earth we share,

to hear the music.

Walden's Ridge, Tennessee 1997

The Four Topical Folios

During the last two decades, my imagery has evolved into four folio categories. Each category contains images that were created in response to ideas and questions evoked by my continuing quest to comprehend our origins and destiny. The folios with their respective symbols are:

Nocturne: The Theatre of Light

For many years, I have been fascinated by the visual isolation and drama that occur during twilight and night hours. Places and objects that appear to be merely ordinary in broad daylight can take on a theatrical panache when only twilight or artificial light is present. Such chance isolations can invoke the tranquil, the mysterious, the surreal, or the humorous muses, and form a subtle alliance with thoughtful communication.

The Gentle Gestalt

The German word Gestalt embodies a unique attribute of perception. A short definition of the word might be, "The whole is greater than the sum of its parts." It is only human to sense the subtle thread of this mystery running through the fabric of life. For me the subjects in this folio had more than enough of this enigmatic quality to draw me into a deeper creative dialogue with them. As I was drawing, it seemed as if I could see the real world and simultaneously a reflection of the world as a narrative of comprehension.

Stories and Allegories

This series of metaphoric images deals with the nature and personality of humanity, as seen in the imprint we leave on the environments and objects that we use. This imprint has an uncanny way of revealing the stuff of mankind. Our love, humor, enthusiasm, joy, apathy, greed, and hatred often speak more truthfully through our life imprint than do our words. Additionally, what we make and how we make it can reveal more about us than a personal photograph. The images in this folio relate to the layering of conscious activity that can be traced through manufactured objects back to humans, and from human nature to our cultural and historic origins.

The Industrial Expedient

Since the birth of Modernist thought in the latter half of the 19th century, Western culture has increasingly relied on technology to solve human problems. The work in this folio attempts to deal honestly and compassionately with the successes and failures of technology.

After nearly two centuries of experience with the Industrial Revolution and its varied offspring, we ought to consider whether technology has actually made us into better people. Perhaps it merely multiplies the effects of our subconscious, and often ethically precarious, choices.

I chose to make these images as admonitions to all of humanity. As we are empowered by more and more technology, we must keep in mind the awesome powers at our disposal and the long-term implications of our actions.

At a Crossroads on State 38 Notes

This self-portrait, completed in the fall of 1988, came from a desire to express visually how I see my work as an artist. In order to indicate the flow of time, I arranged three poses somewhat like the frozen motion in one of Edgerton's flashing strobe photographs. In the first pose, I observe the world around me; in the second, I reflect on what I have seen; and in the third, I look at the viewer, willing to open a dialogue and share experiences.

The theme of time awareness continues in the imaginary landscape behind the faces by including all of the hours between deep night and dawn. In giving the image this setting, I have created a metaphor of my hope for humanity's future and my concern for what seems to be our neglect of understanding and wisdom in preparing for that future.

I was 38 years old when I started the words that later inspired this image (hence, the title). At that time I was having a conflict between the natural inclination to live the conventional rooted life and a multiplying number of good reasons to give in to a very strong wanderlust.

I drew the image about six years later. After I'd finished the drawing, I added the last three stanzas to the text that originally inspired the etching. The words are a stream of thoughts that show how I finally chose to resolve the conflict as I worked through that part of my life.

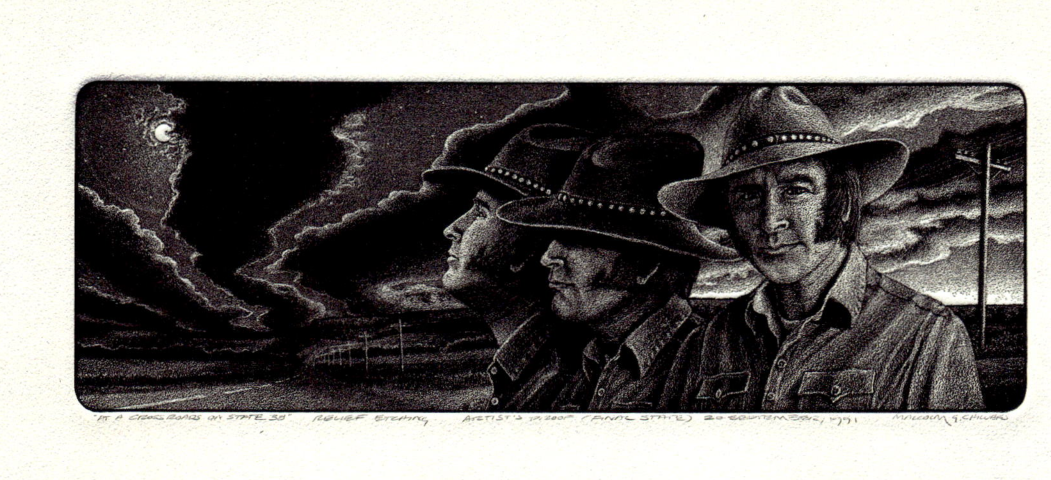

Image size: 6" X 16 3/4" Edition of 260 impressions plus 40 proofs, hand-pulled by the artist on 13" X 20" Arches Cover. Curation completed in September 1991. Plate canceled, January 1995.

At a Crossroads on State 38 (CD One-1)

Odds are you could
find yourself
here in this passage between
moonlight
and dawn,
seeing change
move
through the backwater eddies
and the mainstream flows
of the world around you--
thinking through
choice
and chance,
about things
that have already been
and
might yet be.
Being intimate
with each moment,
and in that labor of love,
you will grow
through the fleeting time
you have left to become
richly
alive.

There is a place
where streets meet
highways--
so many gatherers
pull my eyes,
my mind
out into their networked
webbed souls
stretching on into glorious
days--
the vagabond myth.

Heaven,
earth,
horizon,
endless days of discovery
ending
in grand expansive sundowns;
then evening
and highways meet streets
lined with homes
private,
warm,
perpetuating,
secure by fire

"AT A CROSSROADS ON STATE 35"
RELIEF ETCHING
ARTIST'S PROOF (FINAL STATE)
20 SEPTEMBER, 1991

or television light.
So many gatherers
pull my eyes,
my mind
back into their communal
webbed souls,
holding me in like mother.
Endless days of family
and friends
ending in
quiet porch sundowns;
then morning,

and streets meet
highways.

Heat waves
mirror the horizon,
cumulus fill the sky,
power lines recede
into the distance,
and so also
eventually
will I.

Ahhhh!
Here's some kind
of timely mirage,
Oasis Motel,
gas pumps,
last-chance garage;
transistor deejay
droning over some old
rock tune;
the smell of diesel smoke
in the bright afternoon.

A thousand lives
rush by here each day,
heading back
to as many homes
with as many phones
and a million words to say;
while
I was just
on my way
to see
what's become
of America.

Musical introduction, "ANOTHER MAN'S SUNRISE"

Hamilton County, Tennessee, 1988

Sierra Before the Storm Notes

I have always loved great valleys; the longer the floor, the higher the mountains, the better. *Sierra Before the Storm* was inspired by the Owens Valley in eastern California.

This valley lies between two great mountain ranges. The east is defined by the Inyo and White Mountain chains--stark, arid, and laced with intriguing dikes woven through abrupt walls of native stone. To the west rises the formidable, ragged splendor of the Sierra Nevada Range.

The many memorable experiences I have had in this valley over the years gave me cause to break with my usual practice of commenting on human nature by allegorizing and personifying man-made things. I decided to do an image that was simply about pristine nature.

Sadly, nature that has not been man-handled into submission is becoming more and more scarce. We Americans seem to have a penchant for developing, expanding, and commercializing.

If it is true that we preserve and perpetuate what is most valuable to us, then any casual observer looking at our culture would conclude that unlimited commercial materialism is surely one of our premiere American values.

This image and its *poetic text* have been influenced by a continuing inclination of mine to question the wisdom, the spiritual character, and the aesthetics of such a specifically human-centered world view. My apprehensions culminate in the words of the choral work on the second track of the first CD. The words deliberate what may be one of the consummate human questions.

Will we live on, or will our voices like the silent mouths on images from so many lost civilizations, reverberate into a future world, empty of meaning?

Image size: 16 3/4" X 25 3/8" Final Edition of 260 impressions plus 40 proofs, hand-pulled by the artist on 22" X 30" Arjomari paper stock (240 numbered impressions on Arches Cover and 20 numbered impressions on Arches Buff). A first-state experimental edition of the mirror view of this image was pulled and then discontinued after 32 impressions on BFK Rives. They were curated in July 1985, and the test plate was canceled in January 1995. Final state curation completed in February 1991. Plate canceled, July 1988.

Sierra Before the Storm (CD One-2)

What a day this is!

You know,
I would like to have come
to Owens
before it was known by that
or
any other name.
I would wish for nothing
but to drift with the river,
feel the fresh shock
of cold water on
hot,
dusty
salt skin;
naked
like the fragile valley of life
stretched out
before shaded eyes,
sweeping up
long
gentle pediments
to be bounded
by the hard-bitten
volcanic foothills.

I wanted to live
in the rain shadow
of heavy
east-bound
Pacific squalls,
scraped
by the jagged teeth
of unnamed peaks.

Resting here on the
fringe of cottonwoods,
you can see
the late afternoon
storm clouds
spill
over the spine of this world,
hear the thump
and rattle
of distant thunder,
while the smell
of wet sage
hangs on the wind.

I should have stayed
to see the full moon slip
into the lavender ocean
above the ribboned
marble mountains
to the east
and watched the sky
change to deep indigo,
the monochrome desert
cool,
patterned
like a great
endless
tufted bedspread.

But tethered to the leash
of my obligations,
I was drawn back,
caught in the glare
of oncoming headlights
aimed at Reno or Tahoe
and voices on the radio
pushing
"8.6 percent financing
on all new models,"
inviting me to
"Come up,
Come Up,
COME ALL THE WAY UP
to new improved taste,"
and belting out
with gut-wrenching
obsession,
"OOUUU,
PRETTY, HONEY,
DO YA KNOW WHAT
I LOVE?
IT'S YOU AN ME, BABY,
LIKE A HAN-IN-A
GLOVE.
EVERY NIGHT, BABE,
EVER-Y DAY.
I WANNA GET IT ON
THE AMERICAN WAY.
YOU KNOW,
I WANNA GET IT ON
THE AMERICAN WAY !"

Musical segue, "YOU AN' ME BABY"
Choral invocation, *"DID WE GET ALL THAT WE WANTED? / LIVE ON."*

Big Pine, California, 1983

SIERRA BEFORE THE STORM
RELIEF ETCHING
ARTIST'S PROOF
MALCOLM G. CHILDERS

Nevada Northern Freight #81 Notes

"If anyone has bolted together a mechanism with just fifty percent of the steam locomotive's solid spiritual satisfaction, he hasn't filed for a patent yet."

David P. Morgan

I came into this world during the twilight of the age of steam. The night train from the rail yards at Colton, laboring its way up Box Springs Grade to Hemet, California, was a syncopated lullaby, taking me into an exotic landscape of dreams. Over forty years later in my dreams, I still wander around in a similar but strangely morphing landscape.

Once, when I was about five, the engineer of a switching locomotive gave me a ride in the cab. I was scared half out of my wits being so close to this enormous, thundering, smoke-snorting steel monster, but that experience set the mold. Ever since then I have been a closet steam rail fan. By closet, I mean the term rail fan doesn't come to mind when I am contemplating my raison d'être.

I have, however, caught up with myself in the passion of some pretty bizarre activities pursuing the last remaining steam locomotives, while they were still in the very act of doing their machine magic. I remember once, running hard through a quarter-mile-long, curved pitch-black tunnel in hopes of getting a photo of one of the last big 2-6-6-4's as it approached the far entrance.

On that occasion, the light I saw at the end of the tunnel was not the end of the tunnel, and I had to flatten myself against the cold, wet wall as the train rumbled past in all of its thunderous black-on-black, smoke-choking glory. I emerged from the tunnel about ten minutes later with my t-shirt stretched over my nose so that I could breathe, baptized by a fine anointing of coal ash.

I remember in the mid 50's seeing several steam locomotives, on their way to the ignominy of the scrapman's torch, being towed to their destruction by diesel-powered trains. I didn't know it then, but I was having one of my first experiences with a sense of historic loss.

Back then I would not have understood the kind of corporeal-market mentality that could take these machines, which made their useful work appear graphically enchanting, and with such indifference consign them to destruction.

Twenty years later I started this image, intending to capture and contain my own graphic sense of that solid spiritual satisfaction Morgan described. By the time I was finished with the etching, however, I felt it had become more like a visual parable of the creeping loss of our historic understanding.

A child once asked the engineer of a steam locomotive how fast his train would go. The engineer turned from his drive rod greasing and with a kind but thoughtful expression replied, "Oh, about as fast as we forget to care that it keeps on running."

In this etching, a civilization-building engine, once an integral part of everyday life, has become a rusting hulk for which most Americans have, at best, only a trivial or romanticized memory.

Such losses are inevitable unless we value our history enough to preserve its integrity. I suppose this is where I recognize a debt of gratitude to all of those who extend themselves in the many faceted effort to keep our history as accurate as possible.* Knowing how natural it is for human consciousness to create stories, it is very easy to see how maintaining a credible human record in the face of so many cultural pressures requires vigilance.

Such an effort, however, is well justified; for if we lose the integrity of our history, we lose touch with the great saga of how we got where we are and who we, in the crucible of that epic, have become. That loss would, of course, leave us with merely a mythical self image to do the difficult work of shaping our very real future. Whatever wisdom we have assembled to face the inevitable future has been forged from many centuries of remembering and valuing the results of our trial-and-error past.

If we avail ourselves of the knowledge past generations have gained for us and move forward from their hard-won understandings, then in a way, we will be justifying their trials, suffering, and failures by insuring that the lessons they learned were not in vain.

A growing body of accurate historical knowledge can keep us from repeating old mistakes and having to prove once again through useless human struggle what the course of wisdom should have been.

Image size: 17 3/4" X 23 3/8" Edition of 50 impressions plus 15 proofs, hand-pulled by the artist, on 22" X 30" paper stock; some on Arches Cover or Buff, some on BFK Rives.
Curation completed, June 1979. Plate canceled, January 1980.

* At this writing, Number 81 is in storage, slated for total restoration by the volunteers of the Nevada Northern Railway Museum.

Nevada Northern Freight #81 (CD One-3)

Then,
the accumulation
of billions of days of suns,
layered black,
broken,
ignited incandescent
beneath thousands
of gallons of water,
hardening into hundreds
of pounds per square inch.
Steam
heated the boiler shell
and dome pipes
to well beyond scalding,
amid the knock and thump
of the air compressor,
and the deafening hiss
and veiled spray
of the safety valve.

Now,
heat does not come
to reminiscent levels
on dome,
cab,
bell,
or smokestack,
until late afternoon,
and then
only
by the authority
of the perennial
naked sun.

Then,
burly-armed firemen
with wads of rag waste
polished the satin-smooth
drive rods and valve gear,
wiped the new paint free
of dust and spills.
The builder's plate
in cast relief letters
proudly announced
BALDWIN
LOCOMOTIVE WORKS,
PHILADELPHIA, U.S.A.

Throughout the years
of its use,
the affectionately
maintained
prime mover
knew
no other inhabitants,
save its human overlords.

Now,
mud daubers
make
neat
tunneled rows
tightly gang'd
on the under-boiler belly
shaded cool.

There, also,
the stainless steel,
sticky protein cables
await to trigger
the black,
jerky,
red hour-glass
response.

Dried solid
to every fixed
and moving part,
carbon-black oil paint
like a death shroud
gradually fails
on its vigil
to seal out corrosion,
faintly revealing
oxide patinas
of iridescent
silver blues
and violets.

Then,
hard up the valley,
passing alkali pans,
low
shaded ranch buildings
and endless
fence lines,
the steady
staccato
chuffing.

"NEVADA NORTHERN FREIGHT #81"
RELIEF ETCHING

Thousands of tons
of blister copper
hauled
from the ore concentrator
to the smelter;
school and stock trains
pulled
through the changing
colors of fall;
metered
like the seasons,
Number 81
worked
the hundred-fifty miles
of its domain--
benevolent ambassador
of community
in a vast
and lonely land.

Gripping anticipation
upon hearing,
throaty excitement
to see pass,
the orchestrated symphony
of steel precision

hard to hold

frozen.

Now,
double-bubble,
sticky-faced children
arrange
pink,
white
and blue-shorted bottoms
in a feisty lineup
for a snapshot of the kids
with
choo-choo.

Momma barks,
Daddy clicks,
Bob and Betty
smile plumply.

Having fulfilled
their obligation
to posterity,
they slip
back into the plush
velveteen cool
of the recreation vehicle.

Next stop
Reno.

Later,
a shiny black
Kenworth,
with eighteen
mirror-polished
aluminum wheels
and bold
designer stripes,
shifts gears beneath
progressing plumes
of fading diesel smoke
and heads east
out of Ely
on Highway 50,
running,
fully loaded,
into the gathering dusk.

Musical segue; first verse of
"OUT ON THE HIGHWAY"

Ely, Nevada, 1988

Onyx Store Notes

This place in central eastern California has been part of my mental landscape since the early sixties. It endures there like an oasis of peace and continuance.

Stopping at this old store became a thing I would do, whenever I was driving up Highway 178 into the mountains. I, and whomever I was with, would go in and buy an ice cream sandwich and sit on the bench out front, looking up into the ancient cottonwoods, listening to the birds and wind as we ate our rural market repast. The place was so peaceful that it was hard to get up and keep on driving.

In 1992, while gathering the sounds for the CDs in this book, I drove up the curves of 178 again after having been away for twenty years.

Onyx had grown big enough during that time to support a brand new convenience store and gas station. I came to these first as I drove north on the highway and began to have my apprehensions that the old store couldn't compete and might be closed or even torn down. All my concerns vanished when I rounded a curve and saw the pickups and delivery van parked out front under the trees.

Hey, all right! One hundred forty-one years in this peaceful valley and still in business, I thought to myself, immediately recognizing a nostalgic urge to go inside, lift those white rubber-rimmed lids and probe "around in the Arctic depths."

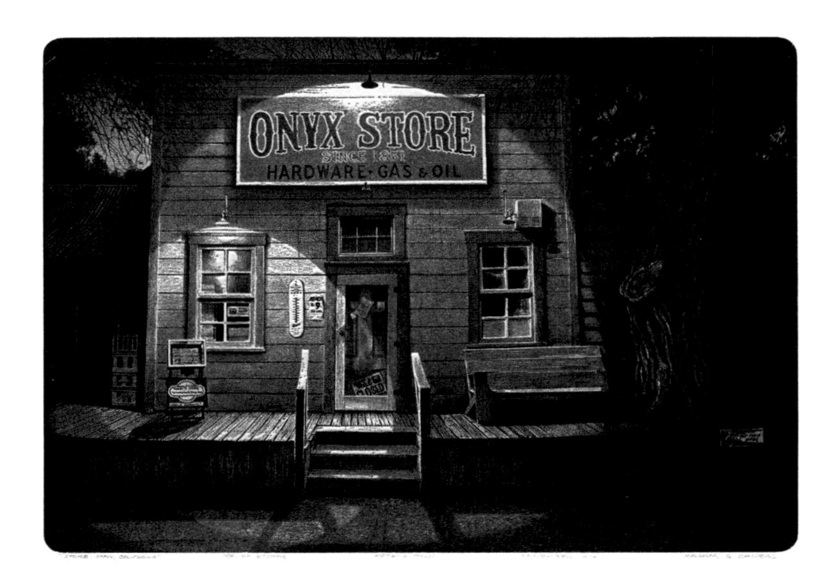

Image size: 18 1/8" X 25 5/8" Edition of 50 impressions plus 15 proofs, hand-pulled by the artist, on 22" X 30" paper stock; some on Arches Buff, some on BFK Rives.
Curation completed, June 1979. Plate canceled, June 1979.

Onyx Store (CD One-4)

The sign
gave the impression
that the store
had been in business
since
three years after
statehood.
The two aged ladies
who owned the place
corroborated
that impression.

Dandelion gray-headed,
they would tend
the counter
to the rum-rum-rum
of an encrusted
evaporative cooler
and
the subconscious rattle
of a top-lid
ice cream freezer.

The naked light bulb interior
was
dim and cool.
The stock
on the sagging shelves,
like the owners,
evinced the weight
of unhurried hours.

Beyond the shaded warp
of the screen door,
a turquoise '58 Chevy wagon
drifted
off the valley blacktop
and came to rest
under a massive cottonwood.

CHUNK! CHUNK!
Eva May's head
jerked up from nodding.
She could just hear
the approaching conversation
of two young men.

"Patriotism!
Hah, hah, hah, ha.
You think patriotism
is just this
flag waving
and venerating
the dead stuff.
Look, Dave,
real patriotism,
I mean real patriotism,
is monitoring
the country's behavior
and doing
what you can
to improve it."

"Aww come on!
If I'd wanted a heated
discussion,
I'dda stayed and
smoked it out
with your old man!
Anyway,
what I'm craving
right now is
something a lot cooler."

Sun-browned hands
raised
white rubber-rimmed lids
and probed around
in the Arctic depths.

"Ah,
how much
for your ice cream
sandwiches?"

Eva May's dry voice
coughed out the answer.
"Thirty-five."

"Sheeze.
They're only a quarter back home"

"Hey, philosopher,
you got a dime?"

ONYX STORE
SINCE 1851
HARDWARE · GAS & OIL
CLOSED

Eva May
put the change
in an old bronze till
as the conversation
retreated to a wooden bench
out front.

Later,
when the lengthening shadow
from the high western hills
had crossed the valley
and made its way
up into
the eastern foothills,
Florence returned
from her weekly Mojave trip
to get supplies.

With a simple routine grace,
the ladies
did their restocking,
including a new box
of ice cream sandwiches
for the freezer.
They turned the store
lights out
and locked the door,
leaving the night lights
burning on the porch.
Teetering off across
the gravel parking lot,
they stopped to talk
with a passing neighbor,
then
bade him goodnight.

They disappeared
into a pink-and-white
frame house,
nestled in a grove of
cottonwoods.
The lights in the old house
went out around ten,
leaving only the moon,
the stars
and the two porch lights
to reveal the peaceful spot
on the long,
night highway.

June bugs
buzzed clumsily
around the weathered
porch boards,
falling on their backs,
legs flailing.
Moths flitted
defiantly close to the bulbs,
singeing,
falling,
returning.
Crickets plied
the wooden cracks.
In the distance
frogs
ratcheted
gutturally.

About four a.m.,
a fog formed
over the valley fields
and drifted indifferently
across the highway.

Now,
just as the night sky
is changing,
the lights
from a southbound semi
appear.

A low,
breathy hum grows steadily
as the diesel approaches
then
EXPLODES
into a buffeting blast of wind,
FLASHING
chrome and red
in the store lights.
Tires singing,
the truck punches
through the fog bank,
leaving the air sharp
with the smell
of diesel smoke
and cow manure.

The fog
slowly rolls in
to fill the yawning hole.

Another day
begins.

Musical segue; last verse of
"OUT ON THE HIGHWAY"

Onyx, California, 1988

The Semi Notes

In the fall of 1972, I spent several weeks doing a personal photographic essay of trucks, truck stops, and the people that formed this crucial artery of American commerce. Back then I lived close to the junction of two major interstate highways and several truck stops.

Gene Franks, an artist friend of mine, owned a barber shop adjacent to one of the truck stops. Whenever I went over to see him, I had a good opportunity to hang around and observe these "Cowboys of the Interstate" and their lifestyle.

Though the accompanying story is fiction, it is based on an incident that I heard about after I had finished the process rendering for the etching. Since then, I have become acquainted with several long-haul truckers. Because I am interested in the accuracy of my portrayals, I have asked many of them to read this account and give me their comments. Their reactions are almost invariably a knowing smile.

Image size: 25 1/4" X 18 3/8" Edition of 50 impressions plus 15 proofs, hand-pulled by the artist on 30" X 22" paper stock; some on Arches Buff, some on BFK Rives.
Curation completed, June 1979. Plate canceled, June 1979.

The Semi (CD One-5)

The work song of lower gears came up the shift lever, massaging Gandy's palm as he eased the aging Peterbilt off the access road, past the truck stop fuel terminal and down a long row of neatly parked 18 wheelers. He carefully maneuvered his truck into an empty slot between a 45-foot Roadway and a red livestock rig, filled with very aromatic feedlot cattle. Gandy reached up and jerked the sleeper curtain open.

"Rise up'n smell the coffee, Beuf."

Beuf rolled awkwardly off the bunk. Yawning and bleary-eyed, he pulled on his boots. When he opened his door, he winced and groaned in a coarse voice. "Naw! Don't tell me; let me guess. You called ahead an' made a reservation for this exact spot."

"I had to do some'm ta wake ya up so's you wouldn't miss the excitement." Gandy rambled through a cocky smile.

Stepping out of the cab, he locked, then shut his door.

"I seen your lids slippin' down there when I was sharin' them ah 'lay of the land' details."

"Yeah. An' I'll bet where you chose to park the truck'll really impress the girls!"

Beuf added with a chuckle, as they headed off toward the coffee shop, through the pasty afternoon light and the numbing drone of long-haul rigs.

"OUT ON THE HIGHWAY" finale' as interlude

"What'er you boys gonna have this afternoon?"

The middle-aged, work-hardened smile of the waitress was glazed in red lipstick and packaged in peroxide hair. She set down two ice waters before the young drivers. Gandy looked up from under the brow of his black range Stetson.

"I'll have a Reuben, some fries, aah black coffee, a slice a' coconut cream pie, an' a goood night woman for my goood buddy Beuf here."

Beuf feigned kicking him under the table. "Will ya listen to this dude tryin' to embarrass me. Dang!"

"And you?" Her red smile had vanished.

THERMO KING
COFFEE SHOP 24 HRS.
DRIVE INS
126402
KCC 345
988 654
85041M
COLTON, CALIFORNIA
RELIEF ETCHING
ARTIST'S PROOF
1 NOVEMBER, 1974
MALCOLM G CHILDERS

"Ah," Beuf looked at the menu, "Make mine ah triple cheeseburger, some onion rings, and ahh let's see. . . I'll have apple cobbler a la mode for dessert."

"Ooo kay."

She finished jotting down the order, turned and rolled her eyes at another waitress as she headed toward the kitchen.

"Well, thank you very much, too, ma'am, sir,"

Gandy saluted smartly, and clicked his boot heels together.

"Geez! I wonder what happened to 'Lotta lovin' Lola? Looks like some mid-life beauty salon got a corner on the menu talent. Did you see that hair and the wide track? Whoa, Beuf, has this stop ever lost its touch for real scenery."

Beuf turned his face to the window to stifle a snicker, but it leaked out anyway.

"Dammit, buddy! You'll get us busted fer indecent solicitation the way you're goin' at it. Isn't this the joint you been braggin' about ever since we got coffee in Pearblossom? Where are all them cute little sleeper queens hidin' anyway?"

Gandy leaned back, pushed up his hat, and addressed his partner's disbelief.

"Now Beuf, would yer ol' buddy lie about some'm as nifty as tappin' strange? I told you there was hot tang on the menu at this stop, an' if you'll just keep yer pants on till I can do some reconnoiterin', by the time we hit Indio we'll both be howling like lobo wolves at the moon. You jes' leav'er ta me."

The waitress returned with a coffee pot in one hand and their entrees balanced daringly on her right arm. She set everything efficiently before them, reciting quietly to herself who had ordered what. Beuf was aware that she was trying to avoid conversation. She started toward the kitchen. Looking back she said,

"I'll return with your pies in a bit"

"Does she live in that walk-in freezer back there?"

Beuf joked between bites of his sandwich, "She's cold as ice."

"Yeah," Gandy mused, rubbing the bridge of his nose.
"I might hav'ta play humble pie with her jes'ta find out what tha hell's goin' on. Some'ms changed since I laid over here on my way out from Georgia last week."

The drivers ate slowly and watched the traffic on the interchange through the tinted window. Outside the gray dinge of transit exhaust turned the late afternoon a dirty brown behind the rows of idling diesel trucks.

"You boys ready for your pies yet?"

Gandy didn't answer directly. He just looked up at her,
"Ma'am, I am sorry about smartin' off when you was takin the order. I didn't mean to offend you."

She set down their desserts.
"I guess I'm touchy about that kina' stuff. I've had ta put up with a lot of it this last week er so since that sleazy swing shift manager Lola got fired. Her an' her little crew nearly cost all of us our jobs. Makes me so mad I could spit hot nails."

Beuf's eyes locked on to her intense expression, "Geez, ma'am what happened? Someone caught with their hand in the till?"

"Till, hell . . . More like someone got caught in a whole lotta you truckers' jeans! Some officials come in here Monday last, tracing a big outbreak of gonorrhea, and the San Bernardino Health Department damn near shut this place down. That woulda' crushed me. I got three kids ta raise on these wages. I can't afford ta lose my job over a quartet of sleeper tramps who just can't stop doin it, and an old Cinderella who always wanted to be a madam but never could afford the house."

Beuf looked like a man who had just been saved from a head-on with a fast train.
"How much business did these broads do?"

"Well, one of them health officer fellas said that just from their rough figures, our little swing shift bordella team had given the ol' standin' ovation ta somethin' like 700 truckers. He left his phone number an' said if I ran into anyone who might have been with one of those sleeper flies, ta please have'm call immediately. I'm sorry if I've been short with you boys. I don't mean ta be. It's just been hell around here trying ta keep this place open. Here's yer ticket; I gotta run. You boys need anything, ya let me know now. OK?"

Beuf dug deep into his cobbler and took a big mouthful. Gandy stared at his coconut cream for a minute and said,

"I gotta use the john." He got up and threaded his way back to the men's room, and stood in front of the urinal in a shocked comprehension of the mild burning sensation he had been feeling for the last day or so. When he returned to the table, he could see Beuf through the tinted window having a casual smoke. His dessert plate was clean. The ticket was gone, and there was a twenty dollar tip under his fork. Outside, Gandy had to talk loud to his friend over the roar of I-10.

"Man, I ain't never seen ya tip like that. Who are you, Kimosabe, last of the big time spenders?"

Beuf took one last drag on his butt then flicked it away. He let the smoke drift slowly out into the thick breeze. Without looking at his friend, he said, "Right now, ol' buddy, I'm feelin' real generous. Here."

He held out his hand and gave Gandy a piece of folded paper and a quarter. Gandy opened the paper. "I asked that waitress, and she told me that San Bernardino wasn't a long distance call."

Beuf noticed the red livestock rig pull out of the space next to their truck, down the row, and into the fuel terminal. It came to a halt with a gasp of air brakes. He could hear the cattle hunkered together, grumbling like convicts in a bad cell. He thought of his wife and kid innocently waiting in their little home in Macon, and it occurred to him that even if the tip he left for that struggling waitress was fifty times as much, it would still be the best deal he'd ever gotten.

Colton, California, 1994

Frenchy's Flathead Flyer on the Right Day Notes

Most social animals live within the framework of an observable pecking order. As human animals, we naturally tend to create and enforce similar power structures. However, with our advanced consciousness, we should be capable of behavior based on understanding, kindness, and respect towards one another, regardless of origin or personal station.

I created this image to symbolize the freedom and potential blessings of a respectful workplace cooperation between humans. In the *concurrent text* to this piece, both the employer C.J. Pinion and his employee Frenchy have a work-based relationship of mutual dignity and shared benefit.

I know that this is, unfortunately, an ideal in the face of reality. Sadly, adversarial posturing among corporate and public employees at all levels is still too much the norm in American workplaces. Although such attitudes are grossly inefficient and often cost enterprises in worker productivity, product quality, loyalty, and finally market share; these old adversarial paradigms hang on like the sophomoric tattoos of youth.

In situations where management and labor begin to see themselves in the same boat and start to work together, the energy usually spent on stressful workplace politics is freed up to go directly into increased productivity that can come from workers at all levels who are allowed to focus on their jobs.

Anyway, there stands Frenchy's flathead flyer. It was pieced together from the parts of many different vehicles, like the potential results of a new but not untried consensus of ideas--ideas about how to create level playing fields between those who own or manage and those who labor, where all are encouraged to do their best work for the common good.

And behind the 'flyer,' there is a landscape big enough to grow that new kind of mutually interactive decision making, which while being sensitive to market forces is less affected by greed, fear and self-serving politics.

On the right day, I can almost hear Frenchy's crusty voice concluding, "*Well, if we can get'er started, . . bet you 'n I could keep 'er runnin.*"

Image size: 16 1/8" X 22 1/4" Edition of 260 impressions plus 40 proofs, hand-pulled by the artist, on 22" X 30" Arjomari paper stock (210 numbered impressions on Arches Cover, 20 numbered impressions on Arches Buff and 30 numbered impressions on BFK Rives).
Curation completed, December 1991. Plate canceled, January 1995.

Frenchy's Flathead Flyer on The Right Day (CD One-6)

The salvage yard at Pinion Auto Parts was as quiet as lunch time, except for a distant conversation coming from beneath a fifties Buick Roadmaster out by the back fence. C.J. rolled out from under the rusted grill, dragging a drive shaft around the bent wheels that shored up the heavy car.

"WHHHHH EW! If it weren't fer them clouds, French, this here day 'ud be jes' too hot ta handle."

A bald head grunted out from under the dusty pink fender.

"UUGH AHHH! Yeah, I'll buy a pound'a that."

Frenchy's fat greasy fingers wallowed around in an old Superman t-shirt.

"Hot days like this is jes' made for the Flathead Flyer."

Bending slightly, Frenchy shoved the rag into his frayed back pocket.

"Boy, you shore spent a lotta time on that jalopy jes' ta have sompin' tadoo on hot days."

Slipping a scratched silver dollar buckle, Frenchy poked the tail of his dirty work shirt over the hefty mound of his belly, back into his pants.

"Naaw, it go a lot deeper'n that, Mista Pinion; the Flyer is my own little piece of American freedom."

"What-da-ya-mean, French?"

"Well, ya know I made it frum all differn't kina cars, Ford, GM, Chrysler; even has a motor outta this old International pickup. Man, when I'm out runnin' da Flyer, it's jes like all the differn't kind'a folks in the US of A out for a Sunday drive."

"FRENCHY'S FLATHEAD FLYER, ON THE RIGHT DAY"
RELIEF ETCHING
ARTIST'S PROOF
15 DECEMBER
MALCOLM G. CHILVERS

As C.J. mused on the reverie in Frenchy's voice, the corners of his thin mouth slipped into a gradual smile.

"Ya know, French, we ain't done a whole heckuva lotta bidness since we opened up this mornin' . . . heh heh Shucks, you n' me otta knock off the rest of the day an take this here ah Great American Freedom Machine a yerz fer a spin. Aahhh, I'll even fill'er up ann'ah pay'ya fer the rest of the day off."

Frenchy looked a little surprised, maybe pleasantly embarrassed, at C.J.'s sudden interest in his time-off creation. Staring down at the oil soaked earth, he cleaned his fingernails on the free end of the Superman t-shirt.

"Well, If we can get 'er started, bet you n'I could keep er runnin."

The labor-worn mechanic's grin was full of stained and crooked teeth. He looked west, out over the rows of rusted and junked cars, and then farther to the blue and tan patchwork of the distant mountain flanks. Mirth tweaked the corners of his eyes.

"Ya know, I bin wonderin' jes how long it wus gonna take fer you ta ask. Heh, heh, heh. You wuz really beginnin' ta look like you could stan' a little freedom today."

Tonopah, Nevada, 1981

On the Cutting Edge of Temporary Notes

In the summer of 1978, I photographed the Medicine Bow Coal Mine in Wyoming. It was one of six mines that I visually archived for the Rocky Mountain Energy Corporation. That job gave me a rare chance to experience personally the heart of a crucial energy industry. When I saw what it took to get at this resource--the miners, the giant machines, the great trenches, the blasting, and the dust--I gained a whole new respect for the value of a kilowatt-hour.

To that experiential respect has been added the difficult knowledge that the burning of all forms of fossil fuel is degrading our atmosphere at an ever-increasing rate. Actively seeking solutions to problems like acid rain and global warming might be the only way to preserve the climate-based agri-economies we are familiar with. If we fail to solve these problems by world consensus, our continued pollution could change the Earth's weather and cause a domino-type collapse of ecosystems crucial not only to existing flora and fauna but to our own existence as well.

In this image, the shovel has not only dug the hole in which it stands, but it is also in the very process of digging into the margins of its own border. This is my metaphor for industrial man at the end of the twentieth century. We are now using up the safety of our sustainable picture. Our hands, empowered by technology, are on the lever. The choices we are now collectively making, whether intentional or not, will likely determine the long-term quality of life for ourselves and almost every other living thing on this planet well into this new millennium.

Image size: 23 3/4" X 19" Edition of 259 impressions plus 40 proofs, hand-pulled by the artist, on 30" X 22" Arjomari paper stock (250 numbered impressions on Arches Cover, 10 numbered impressions on Arches Buff). Curation completed, March 1987. Plate canceled, March 1987.

On the Cutting Edge of Temporary (CD One-7)

Will Iron Heart spat Wintergreen Beechnut from the expanded metal gantry down onto the carbon remains of a Cretaceous forest that was just beginning to show up as patches of brown and black through the menagerie of mining machine tracks on the floor of the first level. He had come out of the cab of the big Bucyrus shovel to stretch the numb out of his jeans, chew, and watch the faded orange mine trucks coming and going from a slowly growing mountain of overburden. It stood out, an anomaly in the distance, like a misplaced southwestern mesa, framed oddly in a sea of rolling and dappled summer hills. He ran his fingers through his long black hair and thought of his family back on the Pine Ridge Reservation, where there was always so much more time than money. At the edge of his gaze, Manolo, the swing shift operator, strode across the dusty tread patterns. Grabbing the handbar, he swung himself onto the steel stairway that led to the cab gantry.

"¿QUE PASA, MI AMIGO DELGADO?"
Manolo gibed. Taking a solid poke at Will's relaxed rib cage, he made a slippery retreat through the open door into the cab. Will coughed out his plug.

"Dang you, Manolo!" he yelled over the growing din of an oncoming mining truck as it backed into position, "you owe me a chew, man!"

Wiping his mouth on his dusty sleeve, he went back into the cab and slid his rangy frame into the operator's seat. "Spala witok," he grumbled.

"Slick move, dude, but you know what regulations say about `grabassin' on the job. All I gotta say is, ya better not let the super catch'ya doin' that kinda shit. Times are plenty lean out here an' there just aren't any free rides on Daddy Coal."

He nudged the swing lever, and their small room turned toward what seemed to be an endless wall of overburden. In the turn he noticed a man with a camera standing up on the edge of the berm, wearing an army belt with many canteens.

"Who's that up on the berm, Manolo?"

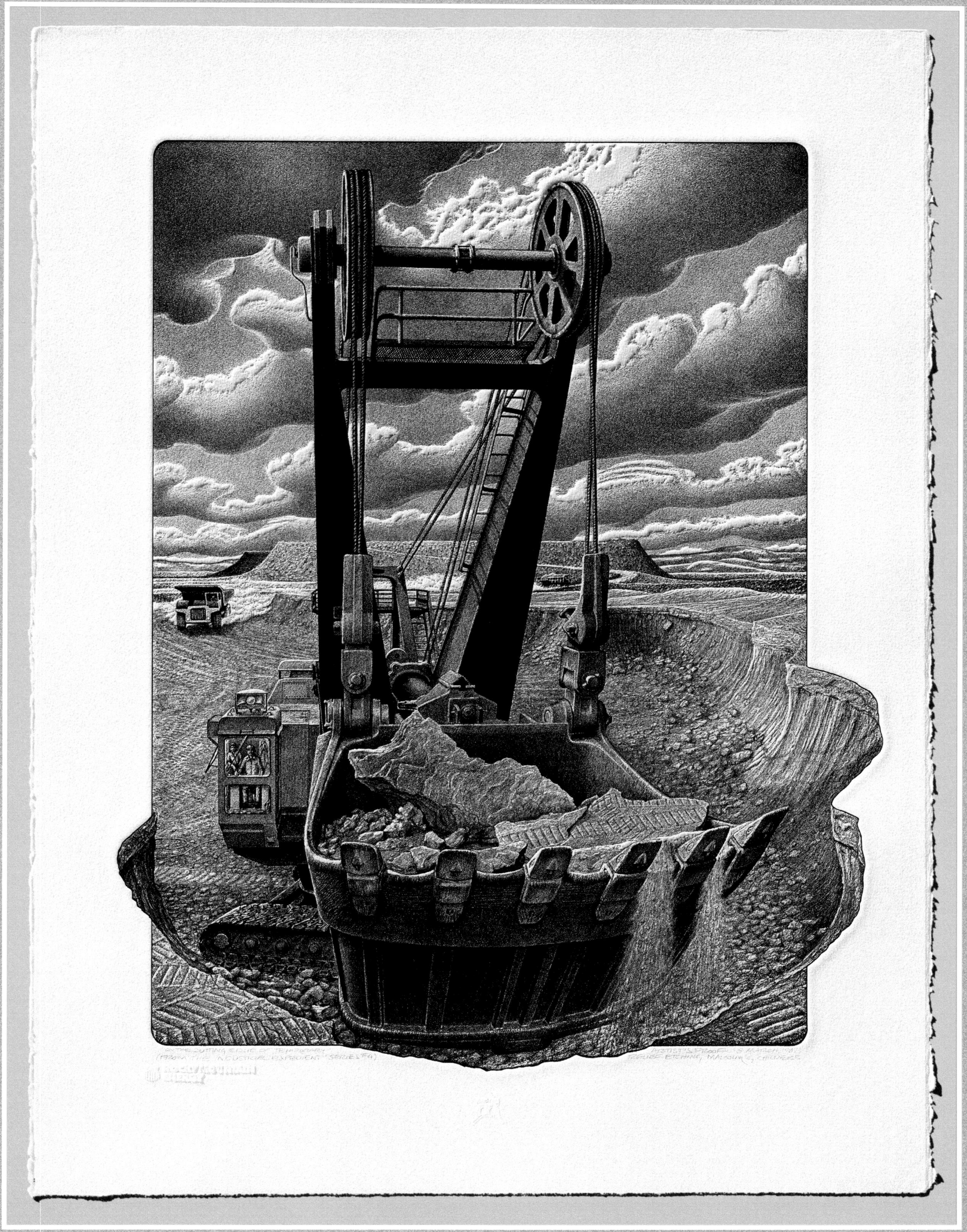

"I THEEN THAD COULD BE THA FATOGHAPHER GUY FROM THE MAIN JUPEE OFFICE DOWN IN DENVER."

"Well, let's see if he's as quick as you are."

Will instinctively lowered the bucket. Cables and wheels groaned as the steel teeth bit into the base of the wall. On top of the berm, a shutter clicked. The photographer stepped back and within seconds the edge of the berm slid into the fiercely toothed maw.

"Aeh, looks like we missed him, Manolo."

"YEAH, BUT I BET HEE GOT JU!"

The photographer laughed and waved to the men in the cab as the shovel swung to dump its load in the truck. He changed his lens, then walked toward the rim of the main pit. Wind caught the dust into spins and eddies at his feet. His eyes followed the sound of truck horns down toward the trench's far wall. The horns went silent. An exposed third-level seam erupted into a fiery black cloud. Ripping thunder echoed in the pit as arching lumps of debris pelted back down onto the blackened floor. Dozers, trucks, and front-end loaders moved in to strip coal.

The dust cloud rose high above the dragline mounds, then drifted away to the south like the photographer in his tired VW camper van, his eyes on the road and his back to a radiant sundown. Twilight was slowly enveloping Highway 30 as he pulled off on a rise overlooking Medicine Bow. The town lights were a delicate sprinkle of diamonds on the hillside.

"Yeah," he said to himself, subconsciously aware of some deep connection in the thought, "I guess there are no free rides after all."

His van drifted back onto the endless concrete ribbon and disappeared into the virgin lavender folds of Wyoming.

Musical segue, "THE SOUTHWIND DESCRIBES THE PLAINS"

Medicine Bow, Wyoming, 1987

Back to Nature Notes

We humans have a problem. The same brain that gives us our remarkable, self-conscious awareness also makes us feel separate from the rest of nature. The disconnectedness shows up whenever we catch ourselves thinking that nature is outside--as in "let's go outside and spend time in nature."

Whatever we feel separate from, we can feel superior to. Whatever we feel superior to, we tend to dominate, whether it is the land, other animals, or each other. In short, this natural glitch in our instincts has put us at needless odds with the Earth and every other living thing. Ironically, the glitch can only be overcome by the critical use of the same brain that originally created the problem. Could it be that the next step in our evolution is up to us?

The military vehicle in this etching symbolizes our all-too-habitual inclination to dominate our surroundings in a self-absorbed manner. The dead deer has been sacrificed on the altar of that attitude. The hunter's stance and gaze indicate that his focus is primarily on his immediate personal concerns, and the natural splendor around him is merely a happy adjunct to the occasion of his "score."

Although the subject of this image is a hunter, it would be inaccurate and unfair to single out hunters as being any more guilty of this kind of separatist attitude than anyone else in the human race. I chose this subject because it graphically mirrors the loss of our greater selves when we arrogantly assume that we have the right or the wisdom to exercise absolute dominance over nature. How much better our lives could be, if we used our mental advantages to live in respectful peace with it.

Image size: 22 1/2" X 17 1/2" Edition of 260 impressions plus 40 proofs, hand-pulled by the artist, on 30" X 22" Arjomari paper stock (210 numbered impressions on Arches Cover, 20 numbered impressions on Arches Buff and 30 numbered impressions on BFK Rives). Curation completed, September 1991. Plate canceled, January 1995.

Back to Nature (CD One-8)

Heh, heh, heh.

Dang, what a day!
I thought I's gonna
hafta hike
all over creation ta score.
I'd just cleaned up
breakfast 'n
started track'n
up this dry wash'n
there 'e was...
fine young buck,
antlers standing out
against the sky.

"Jes' stay there,
mister buck,"
I sez,
as I slipped my Mannlicher
up over a rock 'n
got the crosshairs
on his shoulder,
squeezed the set trigger,
an' breathed out slow.
BLAM!

Second later
that sucker
jes' dropped in his tracks.

Whooowee!
Is there gonna 'be venison
on the table tonight!
Yes, ma'am!
Heh, Heh, Heh, Heh.

I otta have Jim 'n his kids
over.
He ain't done sa good
since he got laid off
at the plant . . .mmm
couple a munts ago.

Well,
it was rougher'n I thought
gettin' my truck
close ta
where I dropped that buck.
Took about'n hour
ta gut 'n pack him down,
an' tie him to the fender.

Been easier
jes' ta stick him up in back.
But then
I want my kids
ta see that their daddy
don't come home
empty-handed.

AMERICA
LOVE IT
OR LEAVE IT

Hope ma boys'll
come hunt'n with me
some day,
after they're grown up
a bit;
that is,
provid'n them
damn conservationists
don't make it impossible.
Where do them
tree-huggin',
owl-lovin' bozos
get off
tellin' us
where to 'n
how much
anyway?

Ain't nothin' wrong
with takin'
an occasional deer.

A workin' man
needs ta get
back ta nature
now and again,
get in a little
wholesome recreation.

Hell,
the way I look at it,
life wouldn't be
much
worth livin'
if a man
couldn't do that.

Right?

Crowley Lake, California, 1980

Ascent from #3 Notes

In the late sixties, I spent a considerable amount of time searching out western ghost towns, wandering around in them and exploring the abandoned mines that made most of them possible. On one occasion, I had gone down about a hundred feet in a vertical shaft when I noticed the strange blue light coming from the shaft head illuminating my hands as I reached for the ladder rungs.

In my third year of college, I made a sketch-like print study from my memory of that experience. The image stuck in my mind as symbolic of the efforts many of us make to struggle through our personal darkness toward whatever we consider to be light.

Later I refined the image and proposed it as an album cover for folk musician and songwriter John McCutcheon. Later yet, I made this edition of relief etchings. The tactile quality of the paper and ink in the finished etching seemed to make the spiritual struggle more palpable, and the image became my icon of hope.

In the *concurrent text* to this piece, the miner, who has long chosen the security of a difficult and mean occupation, takes the hard way out by climbing all the way up the mainshaft to give himself time to face the loss of his cherished security. During his arduous ascent, he discovers his fear of freedom, which has kept him in the dark for so many years.

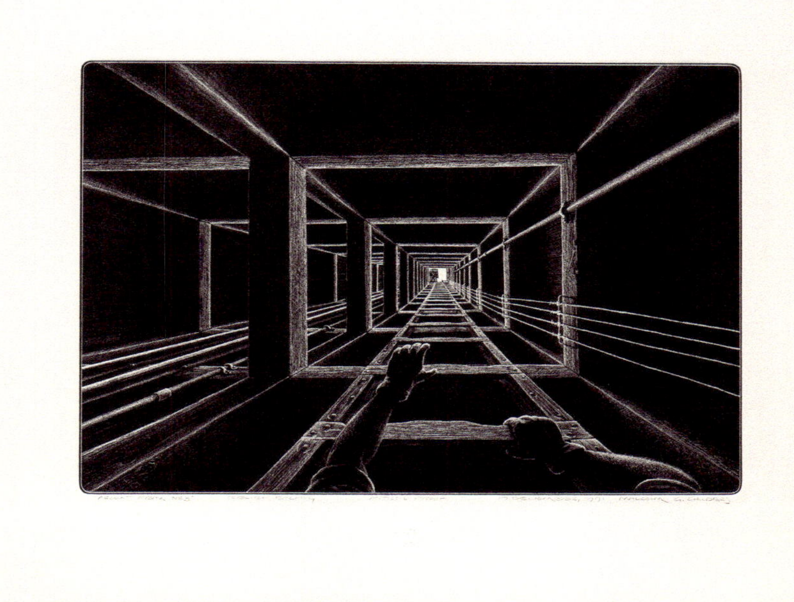

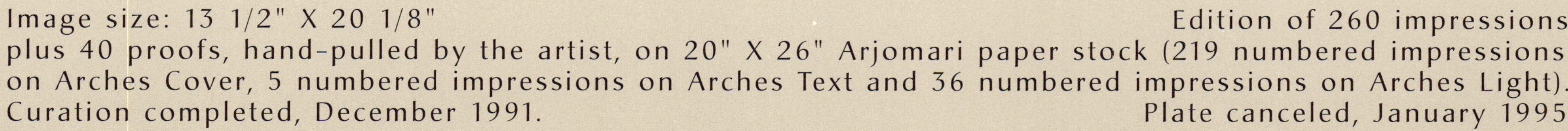

Image size: 13 1/2" X 20 1/8" Edition of 260 impressions plus 40 proofs, hand-pulled by the artist, on 20" X 26" Arjomari paper stock (219 numbered impressions on Arches Cover, 5 numbered impressions on Arches Text and 36 numbered impressions on Arches Light). Curation completed, December 1991. Plate canceled, January 1995.

Ascent from #3 (CD One-9)

This place
Mother Earth,
dark,
womb-like,
has encased me long
with tunnels.
Cavernous rooms
exposed by our hands,
veiled visceral splendor,
seen through dust
by the light
of bobbing hard-hat lamps.

Here a man has solitude,
blanketed
in the rolling hiss
of conveyors,
the winding rasp
of air drills
and the random clatter
of ore loaders
clearing out broken rock
after deafening shots
have punctuated each shift
like school bells
ending sunlit classes
so long ago.

No long lectures here.
The foreman has time
for hand signals,
the energy to bark out
short orders
over the din of business.
Peace comes in lunch pails;
small knots of dusty men
hold postmortems
in the staging area
behind the working face,
always farther from home
and closer to the end.

Having been baptized
a member
of the indispensable brethren,
covered
by the security
of a working pedigree,
or even having weathered
many a layoff
does not dull the shock
of hearing our superintendent
tell of price falls,
large open pits in Brazil,
and the closing
of this operation
in favor
of better investments.

"ASCENT FROM No3"
ARTIST'S PROOF
17 DECEMBER, 1991
MALCOLM G. CHILDERS

The other men
stunned,
pick up their gear
and dolefully
take the cage out.

Still in the shadows,
shaken,
angry,
I unzip
and leave
my parting remarks
drying
on the dusty
uneven floor.

Taking hold of the ladder
that knew
my grandfather's hands,
I ascend
all 600 feet
out of the mainshaft
where this nightmare began;
working off my rage,
climbing
toward the noonday sun.

How will I feed
my children?

Musical segue;
"THROUGH A WINDOW OF DAWN"

Rock Springs, Wyoming, 1978

Amid the Beams and Rust of Days Gone by, We Find Many Another Man's Sunrise Notes

For twenty years this image bumped around in both my photographic files and my memory. I finally ended up drawing it several different ways, making experimental prints of it in a variety of obscure media and even painting it as a full-sheet watercolor with the title written in Chancery hand in the glow of the morning sky.

On one experimental foray, I took the image out to the frontiers of stone lithography. I did a wax rendering of the scene on a finely-grained, medium-grey German limestone. Later while I was in the passion of pulling some really nice impressions from the surface, the middle half of the image just refused to accept ink from the roller.

At the time I had a great deal more curiosity than technical prowess, so I redrew the ghosted portion of the picture, set the stone up in front of a copy camera and made a line negative of the intractable image. I modified the negative by picking the emulsion away with a fine-pointed knife or painting on the emulsion with lithographer's opaque until the photographic proofs from the now-modified negative pleased me.

From that negative, I made two plates. One was a light-sensitive plastic plate by DuPont called *Dycryl*, which made wonderful intaglio images. The other was the photo-magnesium etching plate from which I pulled this final edition.

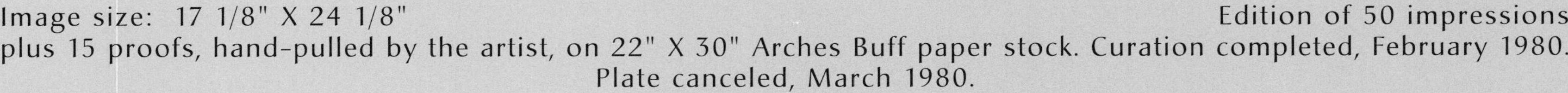

Image size: 17 1/8" X 24 1/8" Edition of 50 impressions plus 15 proofs, hand-pulled by the artist, on 22" X 30" Arches Buff paper stock. Curation completed, February 1980. Plate canceled, March 1980.

Amid the Beams and Rust of Days Gone by, We Find Many Another Man's Sunrise (CD One-10)

I can turn my studied gaze
away from
this sunrise
toward the distant horizon,

but the question will,
like a
latent image on the retina,
still remain.
How had it last been viewed?

By Morgan Flint,
the feisty, wire-haired owner
who gave up deep
New England roots
to chase his
dreams of
wildcat glory
across the Southwest
for health
and fortune,

Or by Seth Lynch,
that burly,
hard-scrabble foreman
he found one evening
out of work in a bar
on the outskirts of Morenci.

Were there scenes of
disaster?
Ledges cracking loose
from a high hanging wall,
heavy jagged rocks
careening down
through many levels
of mined-out vein stope,
smashing
the heavy timber beams
from their wedge
and filling the lives of miners
with dust,
desperation,
and death?

No,
they all left years ago
on a day like today.
Tired dirty faces,
worn-out work boots
crunching down
the exit road gravel;
dinner pails clattering
like a vagabond band
of tinkers,
passing over the brow
and beyond,
heading off--
who knows where--
into the future.

Some yesterday's
two o'clock sun found
young Lauren James,
that spindly assistant clerk
from the Mojave
County Courthouse,
reaching for low gear.

Spinning on through
the sand washes
and dodging the larger stones,
he drove the dusty
Chevrolet coupe
up the steep gravel road
into the rugged volcanic hills.

Then,
steaming,
stalling only half way up,
cussing,
getting out,
slamming the door,
walking,
climbing up the rubble dump,
panting,
stopping to rest in the shade
of the tipple shed,
rummaging through debris for
something he forgot to bring,
and
pounding
with an iron-heavy rock
brought up from
that one deep place,
common to all
of their now
scattered
distant
lives,
to a headframe beam
with rusted roofing nails,
he fixed the corners
of a notice
of receivership
for taxes.

Musical segue,
"COMING DOWN FROM EL DORADO"

Oatman, Arizona, 1980

"AMID THE BEAMS AND RUST OF DAYS GONE BY, WE FIND MANY ANOTHER MAN'S SUNRISE".
RELIEF ETCHING
ARTIST'S PROOF
2 MARCH, 1980
MALCOLM G. CHIVERS

Wooden Mastodon Notes

In the summer of 1972, I was invited by some friends to stay in the basement guest room of their house in Boulder, Colorado. I packed the inside of my green VW bug with enough art supplies to keep me busy through the summer, then lashed my art table to the roof rack. My little car was so full that I felt like Lindbergh staring down that long, muddy runway in those last gripping minutes before take-off on the first Transatlantic flight.

I am not the kind of guy who takes trips just to get there. My routes, if I have any choice in the itinerary, always involve extra time for "rose smelling" excursions. And so it was that I came to be driving north up Animas Canyon out of Silverton, Colorado. I wanted to see the terminus of the old Silverton Northerly Railroad, which I had read about, and anything else I could find of interest along the way.

When I arrived in Animas Forks, I wandered around the remains of that ever-shrinking ghost town. To the west lay California Gulch and the Frisco Mill, which informed this image and text.

What struck me most about the huge wooden building were its timbers. The massive skeletal beams were numbered. All of the structural uprights and spans had been pre-cut to some designer's specification at a sawmill, then loaded on railroad cars, wagons or both, and hauled many steep miles up into this lonely alpine valley where they were assembled. I was impressed by the staying quality of this turn-of-the-century engineering, especially when it dawned on me that most of it had survived about ninety years of severe snow-bound winters in avalanche country.

Later that afternoon, full of Rocky Mountain high and exuberant youthful naivete, I tried to drive my fully-loaded VW bug, complete with art table toupee, over Cinnamon Pass. As the primitive road climbed out of the Animas Canyon toward a summit at 12,635 feet, it got progressively steeper. I kept shifting down and hoping, until I ran out of power in first gear. My 53 horsepower had evaporated just about a hundred feet from the summit.

And, of course, this was when I discovered that my emergency brake was in a virtual state of shot. As anyone can guess, it takes a lot less parking brake to make a car stay put on a gentle hill than it does on a ski slope. I was finding it hard to keep the car from rolling backwards even with the brake lever yanked all the way on, engine off, and the transmission in first gear. That meant I could not get out of my car to scope out the situation or it would have rudely departed without me. That's how steep it was. My heart was in my throat, my foot was going numb on the brake, and I was looking out of my side windows at a whole lot of sky floating peacefully below me.

I don't know what angels of wisdom saved me from that ridiculous and dangerous situation. Perhaps it was the benevolent spirits of the Frisco Mill designers, who, looking down previously, might have noticed me admiring their work. Anyway, I found myself thinking, *If I can just decrease the angle of attack to something that my VW can manage without rolling sideways down this mountain.* Then I noticed a narrow ascending corridor of slightly flatter ground. I turned the wheels and eased back slowly to line up with it.

With blood pounding in my ears, I gunned the engine and let out the clutch. The bug jumped forward about ten feet and then began to die. I mashed the clutch in long enough to let the engine catch its breath, and then I did it again. Through a series of nearly thirty such humping motions in a solid chain-gang cadence, I engineered my way to the summit just in time to meet three Jeeps coming up the other side. As I waited for them to pass me on the narrow road, I overheard one of the Jeepers say, "Isn't Cinnamon Pass Road 'four-wheel drive only?' How'd he get that little foreign heap up here anyway?"

I just flashed a big toothy grin and pulled into an abandoned mine access road. When I shut off the engine and reached for my camera, I noticed my hands were shaking. "That's right, big guy," I said to myself, laughing at the latent absurdity of the situation, "Never let 'um see ya sweat."

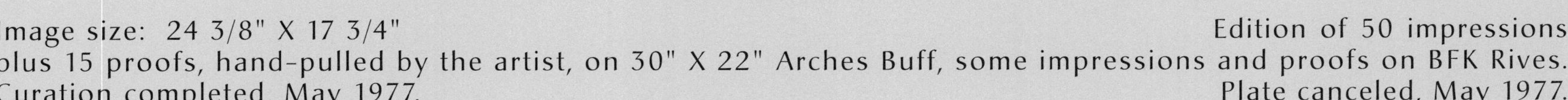

Image size: 24 3/8" X 17 3/4" Edition of 50 impressions plus 15 proofs, hand-pulled by the artist, on 30" X 22" Arches Buff, some impressions and proofs on BFK Rives. Curation completed, May 1977. Plate canceled, May 1977.

Wooden Mastodon (CD One-11)

Mastodon Basin,
California Gulch,
Cinnamon Creek,
Horseshoe Creek,
North Fork,
West Fork,
Forks of the Rio
de Las Animas Perdidas
(River of Lost Souls)--
a eulogy of depressions
worn into the higher edges
of the great Silverton Caldera,
two-hundred-and-forty
square miles
of Colorado
waiting.

Waiting to rise,
waiting to fall,
weighting like an army
of iron hammers
to crush the fiery veins
of mountain building
in the gambling stamp mills
of wealth,
or
waiting like the spores
of future regret
to blow away as dust
from the sour yellow
tailing benches
into the dry
summer air.

Why did these
foreigners
come here with such
conviction,
willing to kill,
willing to die,
bringing with them
their checkered
Christian ethics,
their European
real estate avarice,
their pioneer dreams
of taming nature
and making this
a safe place
to conduct
whatever enterprise
would
pay the most?

In their train came
such an array
of strange devices,
implements
to argue forcefully
their rights
of discovery
and possession
with the lowly
noble savages
and the savage
noble
mountains.

Now,
the emptiness
of their habitations
and this
stripped
vacant
mill building
I stand in front of
reveal
that the easy gold
is all gone.

It has been taken,
then neatly stacked
and catalogued
in secure
distant vaults.

The century-long saga
of what happened
on the thin edge of this
twenty-six-million-year-old
depression
has been
neatly stacked and catalogued
between
the pages
of history.

The finer points
of who possessed what,
who did what to whom,
who did what to what,

or even
who gave a damn
are scratched
along
the alluvium
of the upper
Animas River,

or
are bored
deep into the scarred faces
of the San Juan Mountains,

or
stand
leaning and swaybacked
from the weight
of too many winters
at twelve thousand feet

or
have finally become
irrelevant.

I feel this place
move with my eyes,
knowing the sound
that wind makes
passing through
the talons of an eagle,
as it draws wide its arc
over Hurricane Peak
then
slides
gracefully on conveyored
updrafts above me
off
in the direction
of Cinnamon Pass,
its eyes
knowing the sounds
that pikas
and marmots make
desperately
running for cover.

I feel this place
slipping through
my fingers,
in the moan of wind
through
the skeleton rafters,
and
in the dulcet music
that blood-iron water makes
running
from the Frisco
Mine tunnel.

As I grip
the rust-pitted guyrod
and pull myself higher
into the
individually numbered
fourteen-by-fourteen
timbers,
I marvel
at the resolve
of my barbarian ancestors
who,
in their forceful
passing,
have left me
this ruined memory

of their Trojan mastodon

to play in.

Musical reprise,
"COMING DOWN FROM EL DORADO"

Animas Forks, Colorado, 1994

Darwin Arco Service Notes

I breezed into the old desert mining town of Darwin, California, back in the fall of 1968 and quickly ran out of film. The problem was not that I had failed to bring along enough for an average photographic expedition. This old mining town turned out to be just crawling with the kind of visual stimulus that I had been wandering all over the desert Southwest trying to find.

Metaphoric ironies were leaning up against back alley walls, beckoning like wanton ladies of the evening. Man, I felt like a punk desperado swaggering along those dusty side streets with my scene shooters, facing down and nailing any interesting subject that looked cross-eyed at me.

I was out for a reputation, too, like a renegade bastard son of Weston or Adams wearing my pearl-handled light meter in a low-slung satin-black holster. And then, like getting arrested for being drunk and disorderly, I fanned the film advance lever, but it wouldn't move. I had spent my last shot, my last roll, and my ego was leaking pride like a punctured tire. I slipped back to the cover of my van and drifted away anonymously toward Riverside as the stars began to twinkle out over desert-rat heaven.

The finished etchings from the photographs I got that afternoon are here, entered as evidence of the alleged shooting scene. Three of the images appear in this book: ‘53 Buick Roadmaster (page 91), ‘48 Plymouth (page 115), and this one.

Once I had located this stash of desert "color," I returned many times to take more pictures and talk with the local inhabitants. I was able to locate the owner of this old gas station. His rambling late afternoon conversation inspired the audio drama for this etching.

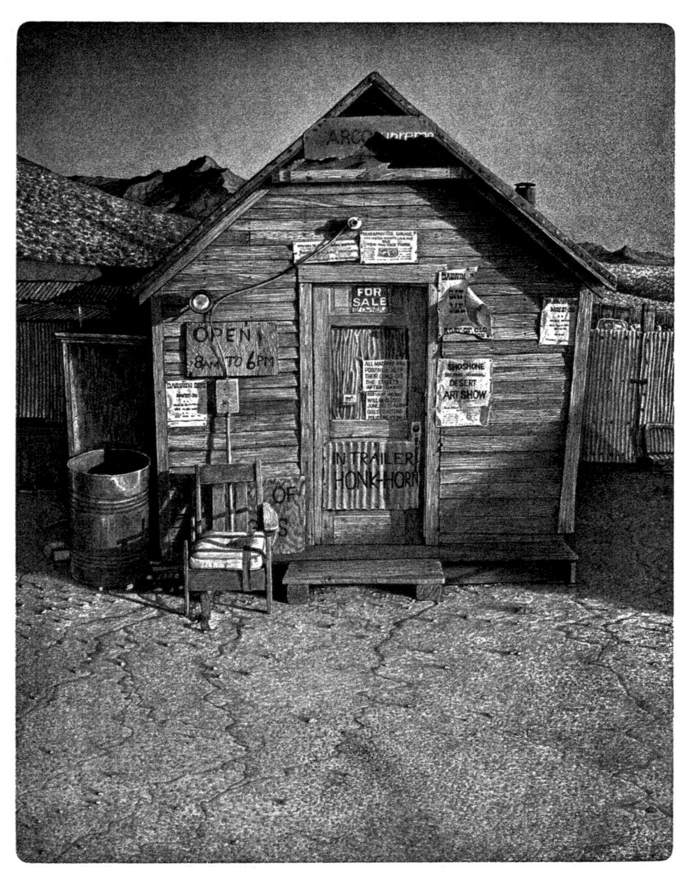

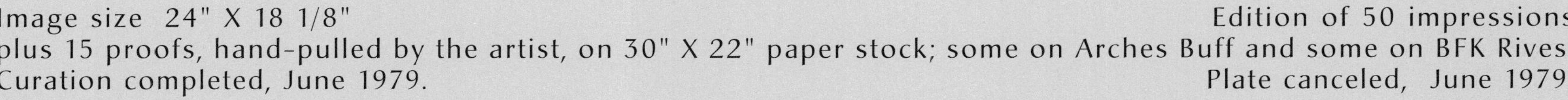

Image size 24" X 18 1/8" Edition of 50 impressions
plus 15 proofs, hand-pulled by the artist, on 30" X 22" paper stock; some on Arches Buff and some on BFK Rives.
Curation completed, June 1979. Plate canceled, June 1979.

Darwin Arco Service (CD One-12)

Must'a been the fall of '65 when I bought this place. The old man who owned it got too sick to keep it up. His kids come and put him in some nursing home down near Mojave.

I moved up here from San Berdoo after my kid got killed foolin' around on one a' them mini bikes. Damn near put the ol' lady on the funny farm with grief. Strange, ya really never know how a death is gonna get to ya'. She didn't get along with him all that well when he was alive. Doc said the quiet out here was what she needed. She's still awful fragile though.

I's getting pretty fed up with the L.A. area anyway--all 'em cars and billboards and glitz. Sheeze! It's too much confusion.

AAGHKK HHMM M!

Hapn' Charley, 'n sometimes Bill, 'n Fred's ole lady come over every once in a while. We'll get that '52 Chevy hood up on my weldin' rack, block'er up level an fill'er full of briquettes. Then we'll lay a wire grate down on top, light'er up n' have us one gut bustin' barbecue.

I'll put on some Roy Orbison or Hank Snow an' we'll get ta dancin', an singin' in the street--laughin', weavin' around drunker'n skunks under the stars. Heck, what'd be a public nuisance anywhere else is just us clearing our throats out here in the middle a'nowhere.

Aahh, I had ta board up the pump a couple a munce ago. The ARCO man said I had to buy a thousand gallons a month er they wouldn't bring it all the way out here. W'hell, the most I ever sold was 'bout 450. It's all right. Me and the old lady get along pretty well on my Army retirement.

I's sit-in' in this chair a few days before I boarded up the pump. Down there by the Outpost Garage, I seen this real jam up Harley chopper turn and head up the street with a biker an' his momma on board. They turned in and pulled up ta my pump.

The biker was lean, had red hair, a long handlebar mustache, and a gold earring in his ear. He was decked out from head to toe in black leather. His ol' lady wudn't haf bad lookin' either. The biker fed the nozzle into his candy-apple gas tank an' I got up an went over.

Man, this bike was wall-to-wall chrome, double-square headlights, long springer forks, a burgundy leather saddle, and twisted chrome rod ever'-where.

Lookin' at all that chrome was like listenin' to a whole band of triangles.

"'R you headed anywhere in p'rticular?" I asked, as he swung his leg up over the bike.

"Oohh, anywhere and nowhere," he replied handing me a two-dollar bill for the gas. He jumped the kick starter a coupl'a times, and the engine rumbled to life. His ol' lady climbed in behind him, and they idled back onto the pavement and roared off up the road.

ARCO
OPEN
8AM TO 6PM
FOR
SALE
SHOSHONE
DESERT
ART SHOW
IN TRAILER
HONK-HORN

I stood there with that two-dollar bill in my hand, remembering when me and my old lady used ta ramble all over like that. She's too sick now; it'd never work.

I felt heavy an' kinda guilty as I walked back ta my chair, knowing that if it wudn't fer her, I'd dig my old Indian Chief outta that shed over there. I'd clean her up 'n polish her till she sparkled, pack my roll, an' lock this place up. Then I'd jes' settle back easy in that big black leather saddle an' ride that ol' flatheaded mother of invention all the way ta kingdom come.

Darwin, California, 1991

THIS IMAGE CONCLUDES THE CD ONE AUDIO PROGRAM. THE CD TWO AUDIO PROGRAM BEGINS ON THE NEXT PAGE.

High Baroque for the Heartland Notes

During the 16th century Reformation, the Roman Catholic Church developed a strategy for reclaiming believers seduced away by the radical doctrines of the Protestant Reformers. Their strategy hinged on the idea that, in the long run, believers are more responsive to strong sensory input than to rational apologetics.

After the Council of Trent, the Roman Catholics inaugurated their new "counter reformation" strategy. The council calculated that it would quiet the minds of the many wavering faithful by dazzling their senses. This religious reaction provoked the High Baroque or Rococo period in the history of both art and music.

I could not help but notice the ironic parallels between this "High Baroque" idea and modern commercial television, a reality of choice for a great percentage of the American public.

In this image, nature envelops and literally swirls around the heartland home, dramatically revealing its complexity and majesty to anyone caring enough to step outside and appreciate the obvious. Just inside the house we can see that characteristic cool light of electronic reality that lets us know someone is home--well, sort of home anyway.

I made two edition states of this image. The first-state edition did not have the smaller image bar above the main picture. That was added in the final state edition because I found myself asking this old agnostic question as I pondered the nature of my topic: Do our senses actually reveal all that there is to know about reality?

Michel Henderson, an artist friend, lives in Colorado and sets tile for a living. I guess it is the kind of work that lets his very active mind run free. He came up with a kind of axiom that I have found useful in my quest for what is objectively real. It went something like this:

Some things are *regardless* of what we think.
Some things are *because* of what we think.
Some things are *only* what we think.
Wisdom begins with knowing the difference.

I think humanity will approach true wisdom whenever we, without duplicity, begin to organize our thoughts and values into a critically objective system and then reconcile our behavior toward each other and the world around us accordingly.

Image size: First state 15" X 21 1/2." Edition of 260 impressions plus 47 proofs, hand-pulled by the artist, on 20" X 26" Arches Cover. Curation completed in December 1991. Plate canceled, January 1995. Final state 17 1/2" X 21 1/2." Edition of 250 impressions plus 40 proofs, hand-pulled by the artist, on 22" X 30" Arches Cover. Curation completed, August 1991. Plate canceled, January 1995.

High Baroque for the Heartland (CD Two-1)

Musical introduction,
"A WALK IN THE HEARTLAND TWILIGHT"

Soft
in the nocturne sky.

"We,
vapored remnants,
the growth
and spawn of storms.
Forming,
decaying,
reforming,
changeless,
ever-changing
revelers,
revealing,
concealing,
sun and moon,
night, dawn and noon,
the heart
and genius of light.

Weaving around
the biosphere
from ocean to land,
fog,
cirrus,
anvil cumulus,
born aloft,
evoking mystery
in our endlessly
evolving presence."

Soft,
through
nylon-draped windows:

"RIGHT?
You can talk about right
at a time like this?
Oh, Nicole,
this is your life.
This is my life.
I love you.
I want you.
How long
are you going to stay
in a marriage with this guy
who treats you
like another one
of his expensive toys?

The ah,
the office
is flying me to
Bermuda
next week
on an assignment.
I could be free
on . . . Thursday.
See if you can
get away."

Laden,
the night air, delicate
with the smell of soil
and plants.

"We,
simple priests of earth,
the growth
and spawn of life.
Wind dancers,
breeze romancers,
many faces
endlessly changing
and applauding
our planet's turning.
Season keepers,
woodland sleepers,
seeding,
growing,
aging,
dying,
giving back to life
our elements,
so that
in the mysterious
promise
of rebirth,
a treasure
like no other is
revealed."

Laden,
the room air, heavy
with the smell of tobacco,
chips, and beer.

"Oklahoma has the ball
on their own
thirty-yard line.
It's second and eight.
Oklahoma's been running
the ball well,
but the Texas linebackers
have been so aggressive
they may choose to throw
to the tight end
over the middle.
They're breaking
the huddle
and,
wait a minute,
it looks like . . .
Yes,
they're lining up
in spread formation.
That's a switch!
The Sooners rarely use
the spread.

The Longhorn coaches
are on the sideline,
so we're gonna break
while they decide
which defense to use."

'Hey, Fred!
Gimmie a light'
PPPUUUFFFFFFFFtt!
'Whoa! Guess we better
make that a BULLFROG LIGHT.'

Translucent
through mirror-surfaced
ponds.

"We,
the blood of life,
the spawn of clouds
distilled,
condensed,
dew,
rills,
streams,
rivers,
lakes,
oceans.
Bringers of green,
frosted in white,
catalyst
for every color of light;
catching,
patterning,
rolling and turning
every view
into faceted meanings.
Awesome in torrent,
fearful in wave,
to all life sovereign,
to mankind
slave.

Yet,
here in this liquid stillness
is found
the mysterious chance
for life to abound."

Translucent
through the color
television tube:

"Friend,
do you revere
that precious blood?
The Bible says
whoever
is washed in the blood,
whoever
is washed in the blood
has passed from death
into life
and will not fall
into eternal punishment.
If every man,
woman and child
who can hear my voice,
would only
turn from their sins
and lift their eyes
toward heaven,
then that ga-lorious
light of righteousness,
the sweet breath
of the Holy Spirit,
and that won-derous
water of life
would be theirs
in abundance.
Can I hear ya say
Amen?

And now
with every head bowed
and every eye closed,
Sister Crista Lamb
will sing
our invitation hymn."

"Dear Lord
you stepped down,
you stepped down
from glory
and laid down
your crown to
be one of us.
And even though you--
you created heaven,
our sins
brought you down
here
to lay in the dust.

Dear Lord
you know I,
you know I
have hurt you,
you who have made the
Earth and the stars.
And though I weep now
when I think on your
suffering,
my tears
cannot wash away
the cause
of your scars."

"Amen
Hallelujah!"

Gospel song segue,
"DEAR LORD YOU KNOW"

Black Fox, Tennessee, 1988

A Funeral For Venus
So Much for Good Intentions Notes

Western culture is saturated to dripping with poems, songs, and stories about the failures of romantic love. Yet sexual attraction still prevails over the more pedestrian values of friendship and compatibility as a basis for partner selection.

Since the beginning of the twentieth century, advertising has used our subconscious preference for romance (sexual attraction) to sell almost everything. The reason for this romantic spin is obvious. Nothing sells like raw emotion, and few emotions can compel us to override our rational intellect as easily as sexual desire.

This image is my memorial to the inability of romance by itself to do what it subconsciously promises it can do, and that is to secure the bond between a couple forever, whatever. Most couples who have lived together for very long come to realize that it is the rarely mentioned values like kindness, grace, friendship, and compatibility that usually provide the best glue for a relationship. These are the virtues that can nurture and sustain the love, which romance may only be able to plant. Without these plain but needful handmaidens of love, all you've got is country music.

Usually the failure of romance, like the failure of any other belief system, requires time for personal reflection and spiritual healing to reclaim lost self esteem in order to get on with the balance of one's life.

I chose an automobile to symbolize the fickle verities of romantic love because it has done more to change Western sexual mores than any other machine. For at least eighty years now, it has played the supporting role of a mobile motel room in the American romance saga.

In this literate image, the love parlor takes on the persona of a hearse or casket. The flowers, a common symbol of rebirth, love, and ironically death, surround the car. A tree, which usually signifies family, growth and perpetuity, stands leafless losing its bark. The storm cloud behind the tree seems to fill in where the leaves might have been, like a memory of goodness, a sense of longing, or the will to continue.

Image size: 16 5/8" X 22 3/4" Edition of 260 impressions plus 41 proofs, hand-pulled by the artist on 22" X 30" Arjomari paper stock (207 numbered impressions on Arches Cover, 20 numbered impressions on Arches Buff, and 33 numbered impressions on BFK Rives).
Curation completed, January 1991. Plate canceled, January 1995.

A Funeral For Venus

So Much for Good Intentions (CD Two-2)

What a rush
of wild flowers,
spring carpets
clean,
bright, and
filled with
the din
of bees
and
other creatures.

What a rush
of wild feeling,
spring feverishly
filling the eyes,
the heart with
subtle expectations
and longings
from deep down.

What a rush
this is with you,
wet excitement
cooled
on the breeze
drifting through
rolled-down windows.
Can this be

love?

What an education
this is,
learning so much
after I was already
sure
I had learned so much.
Can we still be,

love?

What withered trees
can love become
when knowing
is not watered
by the kindness
of patient seasons.

What winter storms
invade
spring's garden house,
but with tempestuous
passing
wash away
sorrows'
clinging to love's
immobile monuments.

Musical segue,
"FOR HOPE OF LOVE"

Red Vale, Colorado, 1984

CLIMAX HOTEL
DANCING & DINING
MINERS BALLROOM
DOWNTOWN ON STATE 91
"A FUNERAL FOR VENUS, SO MUCH FOR GOOD INTENTIONS"
RELIEF ETCHING
ARTIST'S PROOF

Desdichado: An Echo of Stolen Thunder Notes

One possible meaning for the Spanish word des′-di-cha′-do is *an unfortunate outcast.* In Sir Walter Scott's *Ivanhoe,* Wilfred is disinherited by his Saxon father for leaving home to fight with a Norman king. When Wilfred secretly returns after many years as a mysterious knight, he has the word *desdichado,* like a dark riddle, painted on his tournament shield.

There was a strange visual simile between that dispossessed fictional warrior and the tractor in this image which, as I drew it, transformed the tractor into my icon for the plight of some very real Americans.

Agriculture has had its beginnings at diverse times and places when bands of hunter-gatherers learned that they could sow seeds from plants they were eating to get more of the same kind of food next season.

When the plow was invented, about 7,000 years ago, herd animals gained a unique value beyond that of a mere food source. By using large animals to pull the plow, we could tap the richness of fertile valleys on a scale sufficient to sustain the development of task specialization, craftsmanship, and the city building that followed.

By multiplying the amount that one person could produce from the earth, the plow changed not only the population load that a landscape could sustain but also the value that humans put on that ground. In fact, the very idea that land has an intrinsic value is largely linked to its food productivity. On fertile terrains that can sustain such activity, thousands of years of agriculture in parceled and cultivated fields have fixed that notion of land value and ownership.

It was exactly this partitioned land-value notion, so endemic to the mindset of Europeans flocking to the promise of an emerging United States, that clashed with the territorial ideals common to so many native American tribes.

For many native peoples, the idea of owning plots of land sounded understandably absurd. They, with a few agrarian exceptions, had been doing just fine for as long as they could recall, hunting and gathering. The ensuing conflict, like the changing seasons, was inevitable.

In that conflict, the immigrants had almost all the technological advantage. What they did not have was any memory that they themselves had also descended from hunter-gatherers. Within the very limited scope of our written continental history, the indigenous tribes, following European immigration and expansion, were the first of the American *desdichado.*

For European immigrants, the initial dream of self-sufficient land ownership found its Eden in this "opening up" of the American West. Over the years, however, there was a change in focus among many farmers from "What will it take to sustain my family and me on this land?" to "How much profit can I make on my crops this year?"

The imperial notion that scale and success were synonymous, gradually became part of the ethic in our developing culture. That ethic was given a significant push forward by the massive growth in agricultural technology during the first seventy-five years of the twentieth century. These scientific and mechanical advantages gave both the farmers, and those who bought their products, the most productive food supply in the world.

During and after the two World Wars, larger, mechanized, more capital-intensive farms were promoted by government agencies, farm lending institutions, and equipment suppliers. Farmers were encouraged by agricultural authorities to borrow against the higher value of their land and acquire the most up-to-date mechanized technologies to increase their productivity.

By the 1970's the economic climate became unstable enough to produce the conditions that triggered a major farm crisis. First, the market value of the crops failed to cover the stringent demands of servicing the debt which farmers had incurred to become more productive. Next, their land, which was held as security for the debt, began to be worth less than the loan balance.

When that happened, the financial dominoes toppled, leaving not only the farmers, but also the various tradespeople who depended on their patronage, in default and foreclosure. These rural and small-town families joined the ranks of the American *desdichado*. America lost some of the advantage it had by many farmers with their local land experience producing the food supply. With that crisis, the control over our vital market commodities became concentrated in fewer hands.

The agribusinesses that have taken over many of the family farms auctioned off in the wake of that crisis might keep some prices lower on the supermarket shelves for a while. But this dubious benefit has come about at the expense of an entire way of life for many rural Americans.

This literate image is sympathetic to those who have, like many family farmers, struggled to bring their life dreams to fruition only to have them stripped away by what was perceived to be progress. The old tractor in this etching is a Minneapolis Moline, an extinct species of farm machine. It is my icon for the darker ironies that come to pass as a result of some forms of progress.

Here, the otherwise beneficial invention takes on the appearance of a giant insect creeping out of the field, like all the farmers' fears coming home to breakfast. And so it happened in the farm crisis; the new empowering technological means ironically became their adversarial end.

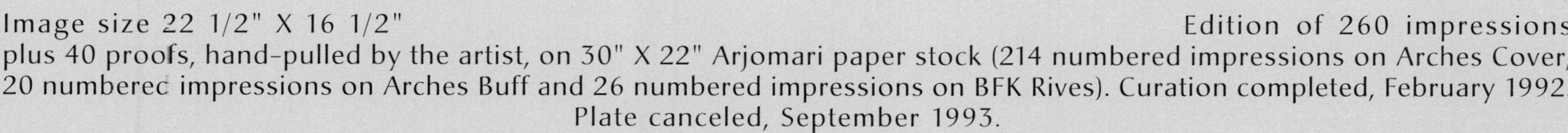

Image size 22 1/2" X 16 1/2" Edition of 260 impressions plus 40 proofs, hand-pulled by the artist, on 30" X 22" Arjomari paper stock (214 numbered impressions on Arches Cover, 20 numbered impressions on Arches Buff and 26 numbered impressions on BFK Rives). Curation completed, February 1992. Plate canceled, September 1993.

Desdichado: An Echo of Stolen Thunder (CD Two-3)

Family farming
is a process
of settling in
and improving
your chances
for survival.

You know,
"Man against Fate"
and the fickle forces
of nature.

To make it work
you must work,
and work,
and work,
and work,
and work to think
of ways to work
to make your work
more productive.

Sometimes
all of this effort
will go well for you
in the marketplace
and so
improve
your chances against
fate,
federal and private
financial finaglers,
and other freaks
of nature.

Sometimes
it doesn't.

If it doesn't,
the beloved residue
of all your work
will be given numbers
and submitted
to some other process
of settling in
and some other attempt
at survival.

And you?

With only recollections
of sunrises
and twilights,
clutching at
whatever meaning
your embattled faith
still allows,
will awaken
to the rest
of your life.

DESDICHADO.

Musical segue,
"IN THE DUST OF DREAMS"

Ogalalla, Nebraska, 1987

Talkin' Durango Flues Notes

I passed through Durango, Colorado, many times in the seventies. On most occasions, I would take a breather and walk in the Durango and Silverton yards, back along the lines of weathered rolling stock to the turntable and the old wooden roundhouse in this image.

The Durango and Silverton Railroad and its sister, The Cumbres and Toltec Scenic Railroad between Chama, New Mexico, and Antonito, Colorado, are all that remain of a once-extensive, narrow-gauge system that played a leading role in America's western epoch. Both sections of track were preserved from the scrap heap by the tireless efforts of many far-sighted individuals. A ride on either one is an experience almost like stepping back seventy years in time.

On one walk into the yard, I turned the corner of the old wooden roundhouse and came upon the scene in this etching. After a conversation that inspired the dialogue to this image, the boilermaker let me take his photograph. When he sat down in the smoke box, his unassuming confidence made me feel as though I was looking at the god of the machine. That event initiated the following line of thought:

> We are like gods to the things we design, make, use, abuse, destroy, save, or restore. It is as if a detectable character portrait is transferred onto the work of our hands. If we are the work of God's hands, then what can we detect about God's character when we look at each other?

When I began the process rendering for this image, I was captivated by such formal design elements as the circle of the boiler firmly couched in the incrementally receding interior volume of the roundhouse room. The weighty triangular mass of the locomotive, firmly based on its pilot beam, catcher and foot plates, seemed to hover a few inches off the ground in contradiction to its own gravity.

There was an interesting range of textures and patterns which, if managed well, could generate a visual gestalt well beyond the subject qualities of the image. All of these aesthetic properties, plus my boyhood affection for this genre of subject matter, gave this piece priority in my large stack of waiting possibilities.

A nagging problem cropped up about fifty hours into the drawing. The problem reminded me that a photograph has, up until recently, enjoyed a certain documentary authority, which can lure the artist who is using one for technical accuracy into the swamps of visual complacency. After you have spent serious time doing your interpretation of that image, however, even the minor difficulties that you blew off as if they were nothing can come back and make you feel like you are up to your arm pits in visual alligators.

The nemesis in this image was the smoke box cover, swung out on its hinges. The visual mass of the cover seriously upset the balance of the drawing. I should have seen the two eyes and big toothy grin of this problem coming toward me before I got into the process rendering and corrected it with thumbnail sketches.

With the boiler circle acting like a visual axle, the whole drawing looked as if it were about to fall clockwise. I added some likely historic props to shore up the listing image. That didn't work. I altered the chiaroscuro densities, but it still looked as if my drawing had a flat tire.

Finally, in the heat of creative desperation, I moved various-sized pieces of white paper around in the upper left-hand corner of my coquille du noir process rendering, searching for the stabilization point like a tire man balancing a wheel with lead weights.

Voila! After determining the exact balance points and the optimum size and shape of the necessary visual white-mass, I added shop lights and electrical conduit, and the visual torque in the image leveled out like a race car coming out of a high-banked turn onto the straightaway.

I am telling on myself here because there may be another artist out there somewhere who would like to know how to avoid such problems or who might already know how to avoid them and just wants to have a good laugh.

Although I was satisfied with my drawing, the experience left me wondering which material God might choose to balance His creation, were He inclined to do so, paper or lead.

Image size: 22 3/8" X 17 1/2" Edition of 250 impressions plus 40 proofs, hand-pulled by the artist, on 30" X 22" Arches Cover. Curation completed, April 1991. Plate canceled, January 1995.

Talkin' Durango Flues (CD Two-4)

TICK-PPFFSSSPOP, NICKIT-PFFFSSNAPP, NICKIT-PPFFFSSSIP, NICK-PPPOOFFSIPP, TIK-POSISNAAP

"Auww, dad gum!"

Looks like I'm not gonna be able ta burn another pipe till I clean the boogers outa this tip.

"BAAWRUP! Heh heh heh. Well, shame on me."

I guess it's about time fer-me-ta untangle myself from all these hoses'n go get a bicarb.

"AAAUUUUGGH-HEH-HEH! OUHH! Sheeze, that sausage I had fer breakfast must'a been made outa wild boar er some'm!"

Little Peaches is gonna hafta change her brand'er they'll be shovin me in the shop fer boiler overhaul. Heh heh, IN-DI-GESTION. Heh heh.

"Say, I'll bet that's what this old wrought iron momma had when they pushed her in here."

An' frum the look of the flues I been pullin, no wonder; carbon, calcium an rust up the ol' ying.

"Whew! *sniff.* well."

Boiler man gets down off the pilot beam

"NAGHH, AHA-ARRRGGHH-murraaat-EH-EH-AAHH-AH-AAAHH!"

Boy it sure feels good ta stretch after being hunkered over with the flues all morning.

"Hmmm, is that bicarb in my truck"

'er in the john?

"OH! I didn't see you there. Most folks don't bother ta come all the way back here."

"Am I not supposed to be here?"

"Nah, I don't mind. Jes be careful."

"Been doin a little boiler work, eh?"

"Yeah, we're fixin the old lady's flues."

"Isn't this locomotive one of those Baldwins that the Denver and Rio Grande got back in the late thirties?"

"Naw, I think the maker's plate on this 'un says 1923. I guess you could tell she's

478
DURANGO
"TAKIN' DURANGO FLUES" RELIEF ETCHING ARTIST'S PROOF 20 APRIL, 1991 MALCOLM G. CHILDERS

gone the second mile from the skew of her catcher. I've even had ta make a couple a them catchers ma'self. Welded 'em up outa old boiler tubes. She's a venerable ol gal long as we keep'r up anyway. Say, heh heh, that's some honkin big camera you got. You with a magazine er newspaper er some'm?"

"No, I'm an artist."

"Oh! ya gonna paint a pi'ture?"

"I might someday, but right now I'm just taking pictures of Americans at their work. Would you mind if I ah got one of you?"

"Well, I cunn see why yu'd want a pi'ture of the engine, but why in heaven's name would you want me in it?"

"Maybe a picture of you doing what you do would show what it's been like to keep these iron ponies running for the last hundred years."

"Well if yaput it that way."

"Can I get one of you up in the boiler?"

"Oh! Heh heh. Ya want me backup're where I was."

"If that's not too much trouble."

"Ah! no trouble, no trouble at all."

Mechanic climbs back up on the pilot beam, picks up his torch, and sits down in the boiler.

"Uughhh . . . Ngehhh!"

"Hey, now! W-wait a minute before you shoot. God knows I'd better warn ya. Heh heh heh heh. This'll probably bust yer camera!" Heh heh heh heh heh.

Musical segue, "BACKROAD BAGATELLE"

Durango, Colorado, 1988

The Flatcar, Blanca, Colorado Notes

There is a mystery in the lines humans draw. Perhaps this mystery, like any other enigma, comes from our subconscious mind wanting to generate meaning wherever it seems to be absent.

During the early years of this century, it was still being argued in astronomic circles that the straight lines on the surface of the planet Mars were water canals. This assertion was then used to support the already burgeoning notion of extraterrestrial intelligent life, which in turn spawned an entire genre known as science fiction.

I am very susceptible to the mystery of lines as artifact. Recently Pam and I spent some time during a ramble through Wyoming tracing the Oregon Trail. We crossed over the trail on the highway several times but finally stood on a dramatic section of the great pioneer road. It was a shallow depression approximately two feet deep, sixty feet wide and 2,000 miles long, made by the steel-rimmed wheels of over 100,000 wagons. During the height of the migration, it was reported that the dust rising from the longer groups of wagons was almost unbearable to those making the journey.

As I stood in the middle of the depression, I tried to imagine the faith and effort required to make such a trek. The emotional effect of visualizing that line, being drawn by the will and bravery of so many, was moving beyond mere nostalgia.

The San Luis Valley Southern Railroad had a similar effect on me. It was a rusted rail sentence written out onto the void of a high sage valley in southern Colorado with one lone flatcar standing at the end like a period. Even that sentence has disappeared now. Only the long, straight grade scar and memories like these remain.

Image size: 24 1/2" X 18 1/4" Edition of 50 impressions plus 15 proofs, hand-pulled by the artist, on 30" X 22" paper stock; some Arches Buff, some on BFK Rives.
Curation completed, June 1979. Plate canceled, June 1979.

The Flatcar, Blanca, Colorado (CD Two-5)

This vacant grade runs
straight south for
eighteen miles or so
beside a gravel road.

Beyond that,
it's hard to tell
where it went
or why.

Of the strange places
that
hang around
my streetlight thoughts,
like
bikers at a bar
on the outskirts,
this one
has stayed with me
well past closing time.

I will let it remain,
drawing me into its
pregnant emptiness
as
I have also drawn it
onto the finely textured
surface
of my memory.

You could begin
the way I saw it first,
standing near the rabbit
brush
on the sweeping
wye junction
with the Rio Grande;
the blustery June sky
adrift across
the high chenille plain
flowing
around and through
the deserted packing sheds,
the wind
moaning in the power lines,
the buildings
squeaking and rattling
over the occasional
faint droning
of a semi passing
on U.S. 160.

My school friends and I,
fresh from a boisterous
lunch
under the Blanca store
cottonwoods,
our laughing,
burping,
sardine breath
brought up short
by the scene before us,
considered
this litany of
disillusioned intentions.
Strewn along
the remaining mile
of worn undulating rails
stood:

two homemade
diesel locomotives,
one with
THE SAN LUIS VALLEY
SOUTHERN
RAILROAD COMPANY
proudly fading
in aluminum paint
on the cab;

the carcass
of a steam locomotive
and tender,
stripped to the bone,
now
only rusting studs
and cylindrical cavities;

a livestock car
with archbar trucks
from the last turn
of a century--
listing
slightly to the east;

an unusual drover's
caboose
with nails
migrating slowly
out of the gray
paintless slats
in regimented rows
dark brown with oxide;

and

the flatcar
standing
where the crews had,
for some reason,
stopped
ripping up the rails,
leaving
only this haunting visage
of transit
remaining.

You could end
the way I saw it last,
driving north past
the flaking abandoned
depot at San Acacio,
hunkered over
with only a promise
of warmth
from the heater
in my old VW camper
van,

along the miles
of snow-rimmed gravel
in late December.
Then stopping,

you also

could stand wide
on the rotting timbers
of the flatcar
and change the lens
on the big camera
to a 55 millimeter
wide angle,
hands
in half-fingered
wool gloves,
aching,
half-frozen
in the 10 below
wind chill,

and

blaze away
at the landscape
like a desperado,
hoping
to bring back
something
that might distill
the mystery
of this strangely stunted
iron road

with its
dream-time
debris,
the diversely
patterned expanse
of the broad
sage plain,

and

rising up slowly
on the valley's
eastern rim,

the massive
enduring faces
of the
Sangre De Cristo Range,
spilling
lavender tails
of winded snow
off
of their 14,000 foot
peaks
into a perfect

steel blue

twilight.

Musical segue,
"A VIEW ON WHITE MOUNTAINS"

Blanca, Colorado, 1994

The Rock Island Line Near Its Vanishing Point Notes

This literate image is both an economic parable and an elegy for a Great Plains railroad. The unpaved county road connecting ranches, farms, and small towns is crossed and superseded by the capital-intensive railroad. The dirt road is maintained by a common tax base for the simple utility of the county people. The railroad is funded by customer shippers as long as there are enough shipments to make capital-intensive efficiency profitable.

A county road maintenance snowplow has crossed the railroad grade. In its routine passing, it has indifferently pushed a ledge of snow up, blocking the rails like a dare to capital commerce.

For no other reason than the simple romance of it, I can fantasize a massive steam locomotive, pulling a fast express that could blast through the ledge knocking that chip off the shoulder of simple utility; but that would accord the profit motive a virtue it does not have.

I find it ironic that some of the same railroads, which played a crucial part in the growth and development of this nation, were built and run by those so familiar with the shady side of business.

Nevertheless, when it comes to moving freight, steel wheels on rail have a significant efficiency advantage over rubber tires on pavement. In fact, it takes twenty times more energy to move the same weight in a truck on the highway than it does on a railroad. Yet in spite of their colorful and costly history, the great tree-like canopy of our steel roads is being abandoned or torn up, until only a shadow of its former reach remains.

I can imagine an American populace with enough thoughtful regard for their history and future, who would have considered many of these irreplaceable limbs of much greater value than the price of scrap steel and used ties for their gardens. But again, that would accord the profit motive a virtue it does not have.

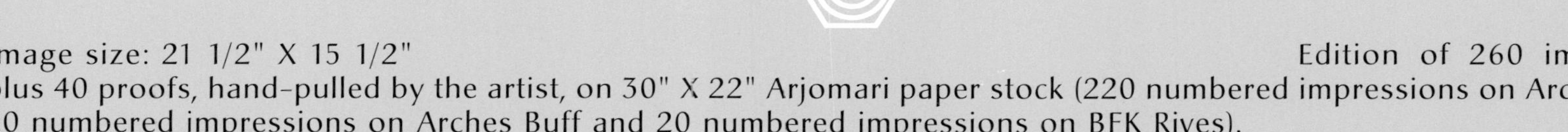

Image size: 21 1/2" X 15 1/2" Edition of 260 impressions plus 40 proofs, hand-pulled by the artist, on 30" X 22" Arjomari paper stock (220 numbered impressions on Arches Cover, 20 numbered impressions on Arches Buff and 20 numbered impressions on BFK Rives).
Curation completed, August 1991. Plate canceled, January 1995.

The Rock Island Line Near Its Vanishing Point (CD Two-6)

X
marks the spot
where
two lines cross.

One,
lightly sketched
by the wagon wheels
of
early high plains
homesteaders,
then
later
cleaned up
and darkened
by the county.

The other line,
planned
with precision
instruments,
was cut,
curved,
and filled
not to exceed
specified gradients,
engineered to yield
the greatest profit
per-ton-mile,
and laid down
like a grand
steel engraving,
systematically embellished
with endless pattern,
and all

very corporate.

From high
over the frostbitten
rangeland
of El Paso County,
you can see the two lines.

One,
stodgy,
plods along
like the work animals
who first drew it,
encumbered
only
by an occasional
stop sign
at road junctions.

"THE ROCK ISLAND LINE (NEAR ITS VANISHING POINT)" RELIEF ETCHING ARTIST PROOF 10 AUGUST, 1991 MALCOLM A CHILDERS

The other line
runs with the curve
of the land,
leaning into corners,
punching
through low hills
amid
vanishing clouds
of steam
and a hint
of fuel oil.

Once,
like a child it ran,
playing
back and forth
across the path
of its elder.
Now,
it lies frozen,
shackled
at common junctions,
by an occasional
abandonment notice
flapping
in the late
winter winds.

Calhan, Colorado, 1986

SP Diesel #3665 Notes

I intended this piece to possess the quality of a tough, twentieth-century icon that could adequately stand for the powers technology has given Western Civilization since the Renaissance. Now, at the beginning of a new millennium, I suppose that an image of a space station or some ethereal graphic demonstrating the light-speed magic of computer data processing might be more in keeping with our common collective experience.

No doubt my diesel locomotive's icon qualities have suffered from the same propensity to become dated, which has been the fate of every icon ever made. The ubiquitous reach of railroads has been in retreat almost everywhere in Europe and America, so there isn't that bluster of 19th and 20th century expansionism to give my locomotive icon its necessary cultural credibility.

All iconography, however, possesses certain similarities. One important similarity is that artists who allow themselves to be confronted by the metaphysical enigmas of life have chosen throughout history to do work which for them expresses something about these great questions: Where do we come from? Who are we? Where are we going? Is there a universal goodness?

As long as we are concerned about the depth and quality of the answers we have for such questions, the icons we make to symbolize that struggle and search will be a visual map of our spiritual evolution. And that, in spite of our ever-growing menagerie of outdated attempts at iconic symbolism, is still no small thing.

Image size: 24 7/8" X 18"
Edition of 50 impressions
plus 15 proofs, hand-pulled by the artist, on 30" X 22" paper stock; some on Arches Buff, some on BFK Rives.
Curation completed, June 1979.
Plate canceled, June 1979.

SP Diesel #3665 (CD Two-7)

The armor-clad runner
stood
waiting
for a change--
some kind of signal,
some order
to direct its
fire-born strength
to traction motors'
tending.

Far out
beyond
the head lamps'
oscillation,
the Earth
through
heat wave mirages
rotating,
slipped
slowly from warmth
to the deeper hues
of evening.

Hard,
smooth,
the global face
of business;
steel rail
the net thrown wide,
encircling,
subduing,
accessing the land.
And the land
now tapped
flows
rich-blooded
like an emperor's ransom.

But for whom
and for whose
thumbs up,
thumbs down
will this great
speechless
slave planet
labor,
and by whose
love over gold
will we survive?

The block light changed
from crimson to green.
The engineer flicked
his cigarette ashes.
The steel-helm'd
squadron
in close-coupled drill
moved out in column
formation.

3665
3665
SP
WATCH YOUR STEP
ALWAYS BE CAREFUL

Briefly
glimpsed
as the units passed,
two
stenciled emblems
on their pilot beam
shoulders–
WATCH YOUR STEP
and
ALWAYS BE CAREFUL–
alluded to goodly
intention.

Musical interlude, "JUST IN PASSING"

Staring
into the distance
as the last car passed,
unsure
of this steel road's
connection,

I sensed
that the market's
blind course
in the future
will be our
common,
inevitable
destination.

Niland, California, 1978

'53 Buick Roadmaster Notes

One thing I find fascinating about automobiles, as creative extensions of the human spirit, is the sometimes humorous, sometimes disturbing parallels that their grill faces have to the cultural mindset during the period of their use. The fact that a particular design is put into production, and enough people purchase the body style for the company to make a profit, gives credit to my auto physiognomy/national mindset hypothesis.

After all, in order to justify manufacture and promotion, any new vehicle designed for the mass market must express the ego message of enough buyers to get them into the showroom and keep them excited about ownership.

The Buick Roadmasters from the early 50's provide a sort of benchmark for my hypothesis. Designed and built in the milieu of America's victories in World War II and the further display of military force in Korea, the Roadmasters had the facial grimace of angry boxers married to the massive bodies of sumo wrestlers. They were definitely authoritarian automobiles.

This is probably just coincidence, but I find it hard to ignore the irony that Buick decided to re-introduce the Roadmaster mystique to their full-size car styling just about the same time America was engaging in the Persian Gulf War.

It was that same mystique that compelled me to place this image at the end of the corridor entrance to the gallery space where I exhibited my first series of etchings. It hung there, barking at passers-by like a junkyard dog. I discreetly told some friends who questioned my choice of image placement that it saved on the expense of a security guard.

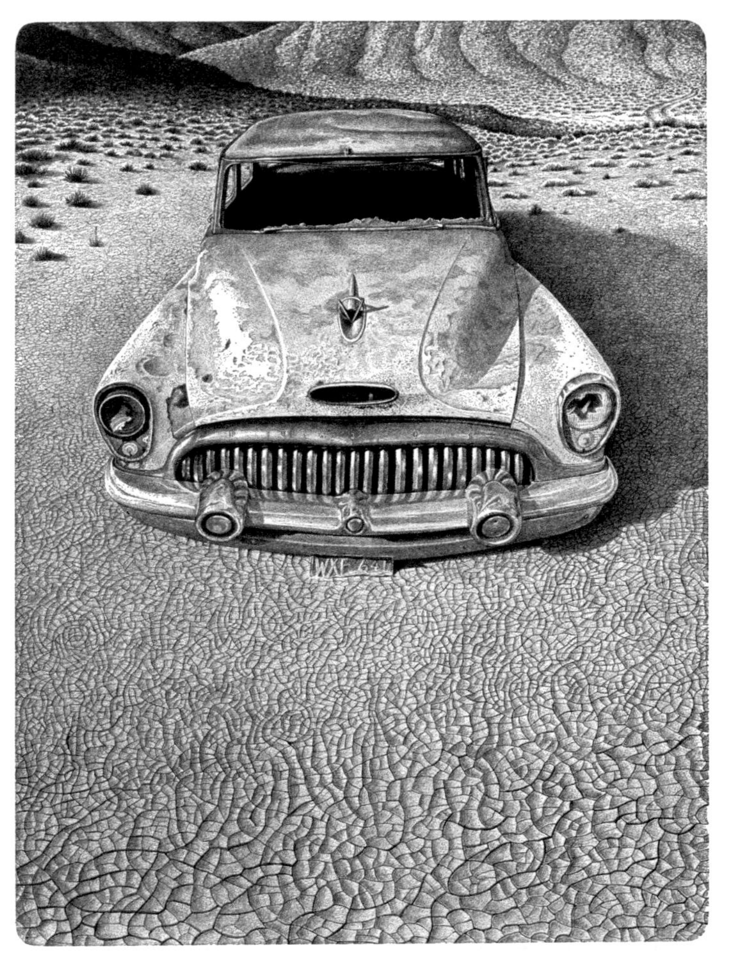

Image size: 25 1/4" X 18 1/4" Edition of 50 impressions plus 15 proofs, hand-pulled by the artist, on 30" X 22" paper stock; some on Arches Buff and some on BFK Rives.
Curation completed, October 1975. Plate canceled, July 1979.

'53 Buick Roadmaster (CD Two-8)

Hey, good buddy, heh, heh. Got a couple a' minutes? Come on over and set yourself down--got somethin' I want to show you.

You won't believe this. Heck--I can hardly believe it myself, but I actually found a picture of Jon Franzetti in an ol' shoebox up in my closet the other day. You remember, I was telling you about Jon a little while back. Well, I brought that photo along 'cause I knew you'd be stopping in sometime today. Lookie here, that's him standing by the landing gear. He was about 27 when this picture was taken of our squadron out at March Air Force Base. We had just come back from Tinian after V-J Day in '45. The rest of the guys there are the crew of our B-29.

Man, we flat had to be one of the best crews to fly bombing runs over Hirohito's privy. We were one of the few to come back intact. It was most likely just luck, but it sure didn't seem like that at the time. America had just kicked butt all over the world, and we were part of the team that did it. Everywhere you looked people were laughing it up and celebratin'.

That night our whole flight crew had a wing-ding down at the club. Harold O' Connor, our flight chief, had to leave the party early because his new wife was coming all the way from Hemet to pick him up. Ol' Harold had had enough to be gettin' loose, If ya know what I mean, so I helped him to the curb.

He said, "Haskins, ina in a couple a' minutes my wife'll be coming up the drive in our '41 Ford. I's a pretty good ol' car, what with rationing and all, sa sa sa don't get me wrong. I don't know how long it will take those Detroit boys to come up with one, but I'm going to buy me the first car that makes me feel like I feel tonight!"

And with that he just sorta fell over backwards, laughing on the lawn. We were both pretty schnockered, cackling away. Then someone happened to turn the sprinklers on, and I had to rescue Harold before he got totally soused.

After that party, our crew was split up, and it was, oh, 'bout thirteen years before I saw Jon Franzetti again. We finally met at a reunion and started catching up on where our lives had taken us. That's when I learned what happened to Harold O' Connor.

I guess old Harold was really serious about that car. He finally found the right one. It was a big two-tone Buick Roadmaster. He and June picked it out and signed the papers. Franzetti told me they were both uncommon proud of that car--drove it all over Riverside show'n it off to their friends.

Well, a few months after they signed

WXF 641

the papers, Harold got shipped off to Korea on some very hush-hush special assignment. They had him up there flying aerial recon missions or somethin'.

Once, when he was over the North, one of the engines and their radio took a hit. They must've felt like they were crotch-high in kim-chi trying to limp that A-26 back to base just as a bad storm front was moving in across the parallel. When our anti-aircraft boys didn't get a reply through the nasty weather, they just assumed my old buddy had dark squinty eyes and blasted him, his crew, and plane all over some frozen Korean hillside. He only had five or six months to go before his retirement. . . sniff ff ahhhh hhh!

It took a long time for poor June to put her life back together after the funeral. Anyway, she must'a drove that great old car for over twenty years; kept it all clean and shiny--sorta' like she knew how he would'a kept it. I guess for her, it was a little like a lover's war memorial cause she never got married again.

One night, some young punks from the southside hot-wired it and drove it all the way to heck and gone up into the high desert--San Bernardino or Inyo County. Hell, I can't remember. Anyway, the punks musta' been getting stoned, 'cause they ran her car out onto a wet mudflat and got it stuck up to the axles. Snif aahhhh!

Well, the cops never caught the scum, least as far as I know anyway, but they did find the Roadmaster about four months later stripped and burned.

I'm sure June got something from her insurance, but how in the world could you insure what that car must've meant to her?

It's probably just as well, though. June would'a had a hard time getting around in that big car these days, not to mention the price of gas. Man, those ol' heavies, sure could suck it up, too.

Last week I was talking to Jon about our next reunion, He said that a couple a months before June retired from the county hospital, she bought herself one'a them brand new Honda Accords.

Musical segue, "REFLECTIONS AT DAY'S END"

Walden's Ridge, Tennessee, 1993

Oro Grande Market Notes

Have you ever looked at a common storefront with the sensibility of an anthropologist, thinking that you might be able to peel away visual layers of communal evidence, like an onion, and arrive at some useful core of truth?

When I was taking the reference photos for this image, I was fascinated by the interaction between what was reflected in the windows and what was visible or obscured by glare inside the darker interior of the store. Also, there was a significant aesthetic contrast between the well-known commercial logos and the local hand-made signs that drew me into this image like the smell of fresh-fried onion rings.

So there I was, standing in the middle of this famous western highway in the heat of ocular passion with all of this going on in my head. I felt as if I were witnessing an archeological event before its time.

I had one eye closed so that the other eye, looking through the camera viewfinder, could compose the images as I shifted around, back and forth from one lane to another, gathering photographs about possible meanings hidden in the layered reflections. The fact that this work was all accomplished at the risk of becoming instant road kill provided me with an experience memorable enough to pique my creative interest.

The onion-layer detective work started when I drew the process rendering a few months later as I listened to the reports of war correspondents, posturing politicians, and demonstrating student activists on the radio in my drawing room.

It was twenty years before the detective work was finished, however. That happened as I wrote many drafts of the *poetic text* for this image, inadvertently exhuming my emotions about being a Viet Nam Veteran in the process with predictable onion-peeling results.

Image size: 18 1/4" X 27 1/8"
Edition of 50 impressions
plus 15 proofs, hand-pulled by the artist, on 22" X 30" on paper stock; some on Arches Buff, some on BFK Rives.
Curation completed, June 1979.
Plate canceled, June 1979.

Oro Grande Market (CD Two-9)

Early March 1973,

I stood
out on the Barstow Road,
old Route 66,
made redundant
by interstate.
In hand my first camera,
the only useful thing
Viet Nam ever got me,
save for a
deepening angst
about the nature of
mankind.

Half-mirrored
by the grace of shade
and the flush of
afternoon light
sharpening and softening
through clouds
of cement factory dust,
the store windows
cast back at me there
in the outbound lane,
the transit-hardened
landscape,
highway,
railroad grade,
tracks,
the devoted arteries
of distant wealth,
and my transient form,
reflecting
in it.

Half a world away,
we watched other arteries.
Our TVs
showed the shock waves
from our well-punctuated,
insistent statements,
ripping
through the rain forest.

This threat
would be deterred.
The patriotic devotion
of our boys,
their youthful ignorance
a surety in service
to the fears of our wealth,
would do this.

Outsider,
what could I learn
that I did not know,
pushing open the doors,
watching their reflections
scroll inward,
like our national
introspection.

Would I be able to smell
week-old produce
over the cigarette traffic?

Dusty faces lit up,
dropping in
on their way home from
work
for a six-pak,
soft economy-size
sandwich loaves,
mayo and mustard,
salami cut from the log,
then wrapped in
white butcher paper--
just enough
to help them get
their share
of tomorrow's,
television glow
and relaxation,
as long
as their health
would let them
without thinking
about it,
much.

Santa Claus
was months gone.
The masking tape
that bore his likeness,
those paper promises,
quit.

He was demoted.
Nobody seemed
to have noticed.

Oro Grande Market
Hamm's
We Will Be Closed
OPEN
Coors
BEER
RABBITS FOR SALE
Rummage Sale
Squirt
CANADA DRY

Many are now
months gone.
The tape
that bore
their paper promises
quit.

They were demoted.
It will be years
before the nation
misses them
much,
and then
only
by reflecting darkly
in mirrored stone.

It was the colored yarn,
formed into zoo animals
on a posterboard
in the window,
that saved me.

There,
directly across
from Santa's
forgotten promises,
in the lower corner
by the door,
below the neon
Coors sign,
the words
of school children
invited their community
to help them go,
see,
learn,
become
the future.
Another chance
lovingly glued down;
hope taped up
once more.

Mankind
may finally live or die
by the strength
of that tape.

From what we
have become,
can we model
for our children
what it means
to know and love
peace,
goodness,
and charity?

Without
the hope
of such wisdoms,
all of our patriotism
may simply be
a more direct path
into the polished
stone gardens
of oblivion.

Musical segue, "ROCK AMERICA"

Oro Grande, California, 1995

First Lessons in Conversational Truck Notes

When I first saw this "late forties" stakeside standing off in a field, I was reminded again of how often we create vehicles and other objects that look like people. After such creations have been around for awhile, they often seem to take on personalities. Some owners end up talking to their vehicles as though any amount of reviling or encouragement would improve performance.

I, perish the thought, have even found myself on occasions mashing the accelerator pedal to the floor in some under-powered contraption, trying to get somewhere the vehicle was never meant to go, yelling with all the enthusiasm of a racing shell coxswain,

"Come on, you gut busting spawn of a vacuum cleaner. We can do it. Close your eyes as we plow this creek. Just think, only a mile more, and we'll have this pie-littered cow trail sucked into the rear view mirror. When we get to town, I'm gonna buy you a long drink of 87 proof and a nice bath--get you all clean and shiny again. Hey!. . . sounds pretty good, huh?"

Ever catch yourself doing this? If this kind of behavior is not anthropomorphic projection, then the words are meaningless.

Well, here is an image with words for all who have engaged in, or haven't as yet but think they might at some future time engage in, the practice of projecting personality on inanimate objects. In order to get it right, you have to learn the language. So sit up straight, take a deep breath and pay close attention because this is your first lesson in "conversational truck."

Image size: 16" X 22" Edition of 260 impressions
plus 35 proofs, hand-pulled by the artist on 22" X 30" Arjomari paper stock (240 numbered impressions on Arches Cover and 20 numbered impressions on Arches Buff), Curation completed, April 1991. Plate canceled, January 1995.

First Lessons in Conversational Truck (CD Two-10)

God, I love this,
going for a walk in a place
I've never been in before.
Yeah, snifffff
time to change the air in my lungs.
Foot cruising like this is
almost always interesting
because ya never can tell
what ya might find
wandering along the thin edge
of a small town
or down a country road.

Sometimes there's this
rich derelict stuff
just lying around.

Shoulda taken up archeology
or anthropology in college
instead of ending up like this
"fringe element" artist guy
who gets his kicks
walking around,
scoping out
other people's backyard memorabilia.
Mighta been less of a romantic 'n
more objective about things.

Sometimes I'll come upon
some old piece of junk and feel,
well, you know,
as if it's trying to get through,
as if there's this other consciousness
beyond the pales of DNA.

Yea, right--ha ha ha!
You certainly can conjure up
a load of fecal ejecta
when you're
all by yourself like this.
Better to opt for mental health
and just enjoy the walk
over this pleasant grassy hill
to see what awaits the hungry eye
on the other side.

Whoa,
would you get a load
of that old moon-faced cabover.
Whoever was working on it
left the hood up and a door open.
The old heap looks so animated
with its hand raised
as if it was trying to get your attention
or flag down a tow truck--
or a cab. Heh heh heh heh heh heh!

Wonder
what kind of life it had?
Guess I oughta go over 'n
check out the paint layers,
see if the pedals are worn to the metal
and the seat cushion down to the wire.
Would it be logical
to put a mind meld on it like Spock?
Might raise its consciousness,
Yeah hea ha ha, and probably lower mine.
What-da-ya think it would say
if it could talk?

A-1335
TRUCK
35:38
78s
FIRST LESSON IN CONVERSATIONAL TRUCK
RELIEF ETCHING
ARTIST'S PROOF

'Heh heh heh
Pretty nosey
fer a young buck, aren't ya?
So ya really wanna know
how this old truck feels, eh?
Well, ya won't get doodley
frum talkin' to my driver.
You can bet yer
last thin dime on that an win.
Yeah, ta hear ol' Axle talk,
the ol' grizzled meathead,
yew'd think he'd done all the work,
year after year.
Steerin' his way down
these rough country roads
chewin' his plug and spittin'
out'ta winder;
splashin' through puddles
when it rained,
an' takin' a nip of anti-freeze
when the temperature drop'd.

Ta hear his story,
yew'd think he's the only one
who ever had to shiver an cough
in the mornin'
before he got his juices pumpin',
or eat the dust of faster cars (cough)
on them back roads yew can't find
on fillin' station maps.
An Momma,
when he'd ease in home,
he'd moan an groan
like he'd been carryin'
the whole world
on his poor old shoulders or sompin'.
Well, I'm here ta tell ya son,
life is a team effort.
Ain't nobody does it all by hisself.

train passes

Aheem AARRuugghh . . .ptuui
Now, da yew want
ta hear this or not?
Tha way yer gawkin' off over there
like sum dumb ol' bloodhound,
yud think a whole passel
a bathin' bewties was haf nekid,
walking down the highway
an hell,
it ain't nothin but a train.
Boy, I' swear
yew'll never learn a thang
till ya pay attention
ta who's talkin' to ya!"

Huhhh,
Di- did I get through?
Ha- have I actually made
contact with the inanimate world?
or was this some kind of
bizarre daydream?
Aaahh,
even if I did get through,
who would believe me?

Ha, ha, ha, ha!
Ahhh, millions.
I can see the tabloid headlines
at the checkout stand already.

GHOST OF GABBY HAYES
CHANNELED
BY MYSTERIOUS
TALKING TRUCK

Musical segue, "BACK ALLEY RIF"

Ramah, Colorado, 1986

Sundown on the Dark Side of the Moon Notes

The tragic explosion of the space shuttle Challenger and the loss of its crew in January 1986 cast doubt on the growing assumption that our systemic leadership in space exploration was becoming "fail safe." During the investigation that followed, the forthrightness of our industrial/governmental complex was drawn up sharply in a mirror of critical introspection. Many troubling decisions set up this disaster. Some of the most obvious were:

-To build the boosters in Utah, instead of near the launch site in Florida. This decision made sectional design and O-rings necessary.
-To use only one O-ring in the design with no safety backup in the event of flame leakage.
-To allow the shuttle launch at temperatures known to compromise O-ring integrity.
-To have designed the shuttle's cockpit without giving it an escape module capability.

When our corporate/governmental hubris triggered this chain of decisions, the ensuing disaster was further exacerbated by the fact that Christa McAuliffe, "the first school teacher astronaut," was on board. A significant percentage of America's schoolchildren were focused on the television, prepared to ride vicariously with her into the glory of space. The psychological shock of seeing this event live must have been intensified in these young minds by the morbid horror of hearing that the crew was very likely still alive when they crashed into the ocean.

During the inquiries that followed the disaster, I could not help feeling that those responsible behaved a lot like children. Each came to the hearing with his own elaborate self-justification and model of blame. My impressions of the inquiry informed this image and story.

The tree, symbolic of the aged human family with its complex burden of psychological defense mechanisms and perceptions, has snared a kite. The kite, a toy that can evoke our very early aspirations of flight, symbolizes the longing to transcend the limits of our own bodies.

The kite string is a metaphor for our control over the results of our efforts to transcend those limits. The setting sun, symbol of the end of an age, backlights the "Man in the Moon" on the kite, showing us his dark side like a parable of wisdom born of pain. If we could guarantee the success of all our struggles for transcendence and always be on the kite's bright side, we would be gods. Maybe we're all just children, trying to survive.

Image size: 17 3/8" X 23 3/4" Edition of 250 impressions plus 47 proofs, hand-pulled by the artist, on 22" X 30" Arches Cover. Curation completed, December 1991. Plate canceled, July 1988.

Sundown on the Dark Side of the Moon (CD Two-11)

"Our local forecast calls for the mercury to fall into the low forties by tonight. Tomorrow morning should see wind gusts up to 20 miles per hour. A low pressure system will be moving into our area during the evening hours on Tuesday, giving us a 70% chance of rain or thunderstorms on Wednesday. And now back to Jeff for today's top stories."

Jason Kinders turned nine years old on Monday. The last gift he opened at the party was from his uncle Sam Washington Kinders who lived across town. Jason tore the cylindrical wrapper away and beamed with delight as he unrolled the kite of his dreams. The kite had a field of indigo blue filled with stars and a plump, "larger than life" man-in-the-moon smiling in the middle.

"It's camouflaged for night flying," Mike observed loudly. This triggered a wave of party laughter and an animated request to Jason's mother. When attempts to gain his mom's permission for a night flight failed, Jason agreed to meet the others at Christa's early next morning.

"Don't forget your kite string. The more you guys bring, the higher we get," he yelled from the front porch as all of his friends headed home.

Tuesday morning was cool and breezy as predicted. When the children left Christa's house on the outskirts of Normington, they were busily discussing the finer points of kite flying. Near the crest of the hill, they stopped to begin the assembly. Jason's voice rose above the others, "Hey, you guys! Look, my uncle showed me how to do this. Here, Christa, if you'll tie these strips of cloth together for the tail, I'll get the crossbars and kite together."

Jason and Christa gave their string to Daniel, who began winding it onto the reel. "Be sure to tie those knots tight," Jason directed as Daniel sat down and started to combine their string.

Didn't Mike say he was coming, Daniel thought to himself, *he's got loads of string. Oh, here he comes.*

"Hey Mike, where ya been?"

Mike moseyed up to Daniel and gestured back toward his house with a very large spool of cotton twine. "Ahh, I was having a little trouble finding my string. I think Rambo was playing bite the rabbit with it yesterday, and I had to crawl in and get it out of the dog house. Yuk."

SUNDOWN ON THE DARKSIDE OF THE MOON
ARTIST'S PROOF
21 DECEMBER

Daniel was beginning to have his doubts about the integrity of Mike's twine. He told Mike to unwind the chewed layer, thinking there would be better string beneath, but it soon became apparent that the entire length might be suspect.

"Mike, I don't think Jason's gonna like
it if we fly his new kite with this old string."

"Aw don't worry, I've flown at least 26 other kites with this stuff, and it never broke. If we want to get it really high, we need to use all my string. I've been saving string since I got my first kite. I got more than all of you guys put together. Besides, if we don't go on and fly it today, we won't get another chance for at least a week, and by then my parents might be taking me to Grandma's house."

Daniel was unconvinced. He looked over at Jason and Christa. They were all finished with the kite and headed his way. The kite looked splendid, almost eager to fly as it flapped in the breeze. Daniel felt an almost irresistible surge of anticipation.

"OK Mike. Here, tie yours on and wind it up."

"Hey, you guys ready with that string yet?" Jason pressed. They waited for Mike to finish, then Daniel held the kite while Jason tied Mike's string to it. The breeze was perfect. All Daniel had to do was hold the kite at the right angle and let go. The reel whirred in Jason's hands. As the children worked their way up to the top of the ridge, they watched their kite climb higher and higher, nodding and bobbing gracefully into the deep blue windy morning. Jason came to the end of the string and stood out proudly at the top of the hill, arms outstretched with the slender white line sweeping up into the blue until it disappeared. Still higher the small spot of kite hung transfixed.

"Ba-dee A-ba-dee A-ba-dee ba! That's all folks," Jason crowed. At that very instant a gust of wind proved to be too much for a section of Mike's old string. An almost silent snap was followed by the gentle, snaky falling of a thousand feet of kite twine. All the children watched, stunned, as their moon and stars were slowly borne away. Wafting, falling, the kite seemed to wave farewell as it sank into the distance. Their disappointment gave way to arguments, blaming, anger, and resentment as the children descended the hill. More than a month passed before they could rebuild their former camaraderie. The kite drifted for about two miles over the rolling January landscape before it became ensnared in the arms of a great aged beech. By nightfall clouds were gathering in the west. The expected thunderstorm came Wednesday morning. The rain dissolved the glue that held the tissue paper man-in-the-moon to his frame. Torrential gusts blew him away, leaving only the tangled tail and the white wooden cross sticks dangling from the bony limbs.

Hamilton County, Tennessee, 1986

The Ides of Gratification Notes

As I was drawing this image, it developed into a carnival of attractions and rejections--a virtual comic strip about the foibles of animal magnetism. In the heat of this scene, I catch the faint yearning scent of pear blossoms, the fragrance #6 of laundry detergent, the pungent impatience of skin bracer, and a whiff of altogether too much old pipe tobacco smoke.

I wanted to do an image that would give the sensitive viewer an opportunity visually to cruise the broadside of an old boarding house in much the same way that one scans a tapestry. As the viewer reads the surface, the image might begin to talk in the voice of the old man sitting on the lower porch. As the "read" continues, a sort of chance burlesque, made all the more captivating by its supposed innocence, unfolds before the viewer. The situation gets further complicated by the suspicious reaction of the old, self-centered authority figure.

In the dialogue that accompanies this image, the protagonist has just begun to focus on the gates of heaven (so to speak), when he gets a sharp rebuke and is asked to leave in the flush of getting caught. With the sting of embarrassment still on his face, the innocent onlooker retreats, saying something tough, using wit to convince himself that he really wasn't all that undone.

In a society that shows off a great deal more than it is willing or able to share, this kind of situation has many parallels. I felt it worth the trouble to show my own vulnerabilities in an effort to identify with anyone who has found himself or herself in a similar situation.

Image size: 16 5/8" X 23 3/8" Edition of 250 impressions plus 47 proofs, hand-pulled by the artist, on 22" X 30" Arches Cover. Curation completed, December 1991. There was an earlier group of test prints pulled from two experimental plates. Plates canceled, January 1995.

The Ides of Gratification (CD Two-12)

"Eeehhh! This road . . . Pfff!" *I don't think it's getting me where I want to go. Betcha I missed my turn back there a mile or so.* "Sniff--Yeah, ol'buddy, time to get directions. AHA! Bingo! Let's see if this old guy knows where he is."

"Ahh, hi there. Ah, does this road go through to Goodsprings?"

"Naww, 'Isshere road jes goes up as far as tha powerhouse. Tha one yew want is 'at ther Merv'l Pike Road."

"O-Oh."

"Yew 'member 'at li'l store with tha win'mill daisies an tha humpin ducks back'ere bout six mile er so?"

"Yeah."

"Well, Merv'l Pike's bout hunnert yards beyond 'at little store."

"I guess I should'a turned right at the last crossroads."

"Ya wanna git yersef lostagin? Now lisun up, an' ile gitcha headin rat."

"Okay."

"Yew gotta turn rat when ya git back across the steel brige. That'll put ya on 30. Then yew go bout five'n ahaf miles to 'at little store. Then yew jes hang a lef after the store on tha Merv'l Pike. Yew got dat?"

"Yeah, thanks for the directions. So, ah, have you lived here long?"

"Been 'ere since nineteen an a fifty-nine"

"Hmm, 30 years. Say, that's what I call roots. It certainly is easy to see why you'd like this place. Nice view of the river and all."

"I's purdy an peaceful. At's what I like. Where you frum anyway?"

"Me? Ahhh, I live about 50 miles west of here. A little town called Walden . . . You heard of it?"

"Naw, don't reckon a hav."

"Oh. Well, anyway, I was just poking around today, looking for subjects that might make interesting drawings. I'm an artist. My house in Walden has a bit of a view out of the picture window, but nothing like this. Just listen to those birds and that sniffff, hmmmmmm, honeysuckle. You retired?"

"Naw, disabled."

"Oh, what happened?"

"I 'ez on isshere construction job over'n Benton, ana fell offa scaffol'."

"I'm sorry. You fell off a what?"

"A SCAFFOL'!"

"OOUUU! How long ago?"

"I 'z back'ere in tha summer ah nineteen n' sebembesebem."

"Do you remember how it happened?"

"Yea. I 'member it was sa'hot that summer yew cud scramble eggs ontha black top. Wez havin a few beers someone brungin fruma party tha nite before. I only had maybe one'er two--I wadent drunk er nuthin'. All of a sudden I'm goin ass over teacup offa tha'scaffol'. Musta blacked out er sumpin'. Broke ma back. Now I can't be aliftin' nothin' heverna bucket a water. Laid me up in tha hospital fer sebem munce. Had me all strung up--wars n' tubes runnin' everwarz. Still hurts too much ta get around so I jes sit heren' look out at tha river."

"You, ah, live in this big house all by yourself?"

"Naw, when ma wife died, ma girls moved back down frum Bluerige."

"Well, it must be comforting to have your girls with you now that your wife is gone and all. Say, I just noticed that rocking horse up on the balcony-- just like the one I had when I was a kid."

"Yeah, at horse is fer ah, onenama gran'kids."

"Oh, how many grandchildren do you have?"

"Got three--a girl an' tew boys."

"I'll bet you enjoy being a grandfather."

"Horse feathers! It's damnear impossible ta get any peace roun' here when them kids get home from school."

"Oh, yeah. I guess they would have a way of getting on your nerves sometimes." *Oh my goodness--whoa!*

"Whachew gawkin' at anyway?"

"Ah, real nice ah, Victorian ornamentation on those ah, uprights. Could stand some fixin', maybe a little paint but . . ."

"I thank its about time fer yew ta get lost, boy."

Can he tell? "Whatdayamean, get lost?"

"**YEW GOT WAX IN YER EARS BOY? MOVE YER BUTT ON OUT'TA HERE--YER SPOLIN' MY VIEW!**"

"OK! OK! Don't get your shorts in a knot. I'm leaving."

"Talk about spoiling an otherwise beautiful view, you moldy old rump roast. See if I ever put you in one of my etchings!"

Reliance, Tennessee, 1988

For the Ocoee and Other Sylvan Dreams Notes

Most of us at times have found ourselves in the uneasy position of needing to communicate deeply personal feelings or experiences to someone. If our communication is successful, we can gain a confidante, ally, or maybe even a friend. If our communication fails, we can incur responses ranging from apathy to passionate rejection.

I chose the visual complexity of this uniquely figured Appalachian river to typify a universal human condition. This image is my metaphor for the difficult work of meaningful sharing. Because the image is not immediately comprehensible, greater concentration is required of the viewer in order to determine what is tangible and what is merely reflection.

The effort required to do this deciphering in an otherwise credibly realistic landscape is not unlike the effort required for humans to understand one another empathetically. Empathetic understanding between individuals, cultures, races, and nations is one of the very first doors humanity must go through, if we treasure a peaceful or sustainable future.

The monologue begins by recounting my attempt to share with my father some of the memorable experiences that I had while walking out on the naturally sculptured bedrock of the Ocoee River. It ends with a philosophic recessional in the wake of his hapless rejection of my invitation to share a similar experience.

The effort to reveal who we are, or the effort to receive such overtures from someone else, is a significant part of being fully human. The willingness to empathetically regard the great diversity in our world is known by other terms. Some of these are openness, kindness, grace, humility, fairness, justice, and love. At a deep and often unseen level, these ephemeral attitudes are crucial to the growth of what is best in any civilization, and they are the final measure of worth for any human society.

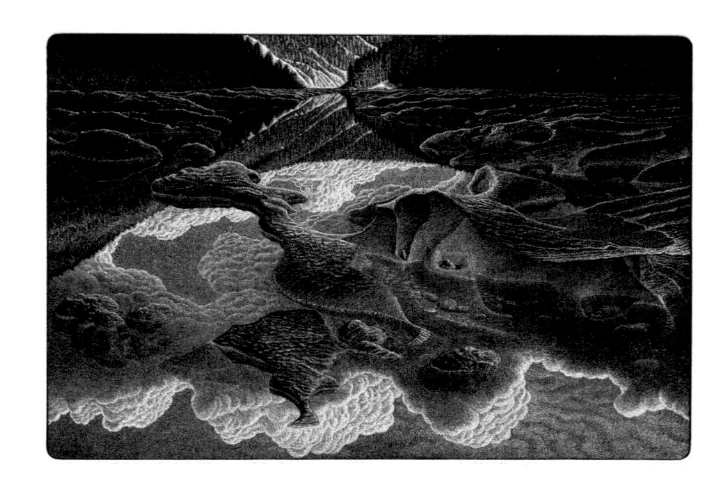

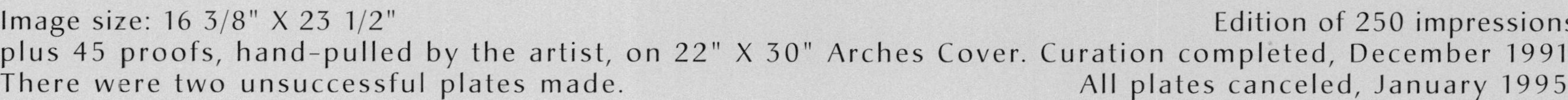

Image size: 16 3/8" X 23 1/2" Edition of 250 impressions plus 45 proofs, hand-pulled by the artist, on 22" X 30" Arches Cover. Curation completed, December 1991. There were two unsuccessful plates made. All plates canceled, January 1995.

For the Ocoee and Other Sylvan Dreams (CD Two-13)

Just up the road here,
maybe couple of miles,
there's that place
I've been telling you about.

Ya know,
having been
raised in the West,
out in all that space
and angularity,
gave me a certain reverence
for life and land forms.

I could see a constant
struggle and submission
going on out there.
Sometimes
the West seems like
a metaphor
for my own
subconscious battle
with creeping finitude.

Well, anyway,
growing up out there
kinda set me up
to appreciate the place
I want to show you.
It'll be coming up soon.
I'll let you know
when to pull off.

I think it was
the spring of '74
when I first saw this river.
Might've been Chris,
nah,
must have been Ellen
who first brought me up here.

In the summertime,
the country people
from around here
come to sunbathe
on the river rocks.
It's sort of
an Appalachian beach,
and there's always
the white water
and kayak crowd
when the dams are opened,
and the river
spends itself for fun
instead of electricity.

Oh, here's a good spot.
Pull off on this next turnout.

Yeah, I remember this place.

Oh! don't forget your camera.

There's an easy way down
the embankment
right over here.
Just let me know
if you need any help
getting down.
Hah hah hah.
You're really
gonna love this.

Why are you still standing
up there?

Yeah, I know
it doesn't look like much
from up there,
but this kind of beauty
can't be seen
from the road.
You'll miss the whole show
if you don't get
out on the rocks.
Are you sure you
don't want to try it?
It's really not that difficult.
Oh.
Seems kinda sad to come
all the way up here and then
just stand up there
on the highway,

especially when
such visual delights
are within easy reach.

Aahhhaa. Well, Okay.
Do you mind if I look around
a little,
say,
20 or 30 minutes?

Just honk the horn
when you get ready to go.

Hard to share this share.
Hard to pass on
beyond the borders
of this frail envelope
these richest of riches.

Our habits
constantly impose limits
on our grasp of reality.
We all choose how wide
we want to open our eyes.

Only a few steps
out on the rocks
and already I begin
to sense the glory,
walking
toward the main channel;
that merging of sky
and land,
interfaced contradictions.

Then
the wind
capriciously
erases the dreamscape
with a rococo display
of water patterns,
dazzling skeins
of spectral light
caressing
and describing
the veiled forms
of submarine stone.

I shall never
run short
of a thirst to see
or
a desire
to stand in awe
of dreams like these.

I am not blinded
in this romance.
I see the beer cans,
the trash,
and
the spray paint graffiti;
sorry evidence
of those who
have gotten out
onto the rocks,
leaving
whatever
sensibilities they had
up there,
sitting in their car.

Why is it
that there are so
many of us
who
have never learned
to dream

with the land?

Choral benediction,
"PEACE RIVER / MAYBE WE'RE
ALL JUST CHILDREN"

Ocoee River Dalles, Tennessee, 1988

THIS IMAGE CONCLUDES THE CD TWO AUDIO PROGRAM.

'48 Plymouth Notes

Dan Landrum, a musician friend of mine, spent time as a reporter for a local radio station. One morning we met for breakfast at a restaurant near his "day job" office. I asked him, on a lark, what was his most embarrassing moment on live radio. The account he told me inspired the short story for this image.

My fictional story differs from his account in two major areas. First, my friend didn't know either one of the deceased people personally. He was told by an officer that the man was an insurance salesman. Second, because this was eyewitness news, the efficient broadcast crew had quickly set up their gear to send his report out live from the scene.

When he came out of the small suburban home, having viewed the tragedy, he was handed a mike just as the countdown to broadcast began. Across the street, several of his police buddies were milling around their patrol cars whispering to one another--some with their hands over their faces, snickering.

Image size: "18 1/8" X 24" Edition of 50 impressions plus 15 proofs, hand-pulled by the artist, on 22" X 30" paper stock; some on Arches Buff, some on BFK Rives. Curation completed, June 1979. Plate canceled, June 1979.

'48 Plymouth

"So, Word Man, what's the story behind this one?" Graham Camp, who for years had a curious fascination with the history of derelict objects, stood captivated by a faded 5x7 glossy tacked up in a menagerie of frozen paper moments on the backroom office wall. Dan Lando, former reporter, local historian and desert philosopher, peered up from the faint cool glow of his word processor to see Camp's finger resting on the photograph of a rather tired looking '48 Plymouth.

"Oh! That old heap." Lando's bushy white eyebrows sprouted magnificent crow's feet from both sides of his half-glasses. "That was a hell of a scoop all right. Give me a few minutes to finish this editorial, and we'll have a generous helping of journalism over lunch."

It was about 12:15 when Camp and Lando stepped out of the cool office into a windy autumn day. They paused to let a garbage truck pass, then quickly crossed the street.

The syncopated rumble of four big road locomotives, pulling a long freight train out of the yards toward Needles, began to engulf the din of traffic. The two walked up the street through the shade of business awnings, then slipped into the aromatic darkness of a little Mexican cantina on the corner. As the door closed slowly behind them, commotion from the outside traffic shifted to mariachi music.

Lando chose to sit a comfortable distance from an air-conditioning vent and slid himself into the booth all the way to the wall. He lifted his legs and rested them long-ways on the maroon naugahyde bench.

"Varicosities," he said, "gotta keep these tired old puppies elevated."

A little dark, roundish woman came down the aisle with an appetizer of nachos and salsa. She took their orders, reciting the specials in a thick rolling accent, then hurried away toward the kitchen.

The '48 Plymouth story began with an easy hand-to-mouth cadence as they dipped the corn triangles in salsa. Camp waited to see his friend's reaction to the sauce, secretly hoping that it was the mild El Gringo stuff.

"Herbert Biggs," Lando crunched, "owned that Plymouth you saw on the wall. He was the first and only salesman for the Golden Empire Life and Casualty Company out here on the desert end of San Bernardino County.

He had a small office a couple of blocks down from here, off the main drag, and lived in the apartment above it from the early fifties clear up to 1962 when I took that photo of his car about six miles east of Yermo.

Most folks aren't aware of this, but if you take into account the land area alone, San Bernardino County is bigger than a lot of New England states, and I'd bet back in the fifties it had fewer residents than Maine. It's easy to see how Biggs might've put some serious mileage on his car out here, following up leads and servicing all his far-flung accounts.

Bones, one of the mechanics down at the county garage, drove the Plymouth back to the county yard. Ol' Bones, aaah. He was such a character. Wish you'd met him before he passed on.

He pointed to the Plymouth with a badly chewed cigar in his gnarly black hand and said with his Louise Armstrong voice, 'Yeah, Herbie couldn'a driven dat ol' car much

CALIFORNIA
VCM 731

longer--da rodsn' mains are damn near gone. It was smokin' like a convict on a cold mornin' all the way back to town, so either da rings or da guides are shot, and dat right front's so bald it wuz layin down fingerprints a haf blin deetective cu follow.'"

During Lando's reverie, Camp had noticed a growing baldness in the nacho bowl. In a couple of minutes the little round lady returned with a pair of steaming oval plates balanced on what appeared to be decorated welder's gloves. She set the food down in front of them and went to get their drinks. Camp wondered to himself if the subtle odor under the aroma of spicy cheese might actually be the smell of smoking Formica. The lady returned with two fresh ice waters, his ice tea and Lando's bottle of Corona.

Lando put his legs down, picked up his fork and went to work. Camp watched with apprehension as his friend launched the first fork full.

"Oh, oh, oh, oh!" Lando reached for the ice water, "Damn, that's a good relleno!" Fanning his mouth and blowing to cool his tongue, he went on.

"Now Biggs, his name was an irony in itself. Hell, he couldn't have been taller than 5' 5," maybe 5' 6," and with his billiard head and slight build, I'd be surprised if he weighed more than 130 pounds soaking wet.

Even though Herbie lacked that dynamic personality so many short men develop to compensate for their size, he had a pleasant sincerity that made him comfortable to be around. He could be jovial, even funny at times, but beneath the surface I could still sense a kind of chronic loneliness.

Maybe it was all of those long desert miles spent between Baker, Needles or Twenty-Nine Palms. Maybe it was a deep-seated fear of rejection that kept him from looking for a wife. I'm sure I don't know. My Ellen even tried to fix him up with a very nice short lady at her office, but he just sorta bowed out with a painfully shy apology."

"You seem to know a lot of personal stuff about Biggs," Camp interrupted, nonchalantly cutting up his chimichanga to let it cool. Lando followed suit with his three rellenos.

"Well, as you know, I got on here at the newspaper back in 1957, and our paths would cross every once in a while as he was checking up on a claim, and I was out gathering news-worthy details. When we connected, we would usually take a break in some quiet watering hole to compare notes. I've never minded an opportunity to kick back in a cool place during work hours as long as it would still fit into my job description. I guess that's what made Biggs more than an acquaintance.

Still remember the last time I saw Biggs. It was about this time of year, maybe November. I was returning from Victorville late one after-noon, and dropped in to see my cousin who had become the manager at a roadhouse on Route 66. Thought I'd be there just a minute or so, cheering him on, but when I walked into the bar, there was Biggs's billiard dome shining across the darkened dining room at me.

As soon as I'd finished congratulating and back-slapping with my cousin, I went over and sat down with Biggs, who was about halfway through his supper. He said he was tired from a long day out on the road, but he looked happier than I'd ever seen him before.

He told me that a Minneapolis firm had approached him earlier that month to market annuities to teachers. He was very excited about the plan's potential, and though he hadn't been trying to sell the annuities all that long, he assured me that he would soon trade his old Plymouth in on a flashy new Buick.

I told him it was about time he got a break and wished him all the luck in the world. When he sensed I was about to get up and head on home, he looked like he wanted to say more, so I asked him if that was the only reason he was smiling. He looked taken aback, like he'd just caught me picking his pockets, then admitted shyly that there was another reason for his happiness.

At first he didn't know if he should trust me with this new secret, being as how my business was news, so he made me swear on my honor not to tell a soul. When I gave him my word, he said that he had been spending time with a lady and felt very comfortable about the way it was going. I eased back into the chair, not believing what I had just heard.

Here is this precise little guy who's been a bachelor for about fifty-five years telling me like a school kid that he's found a girlfriend. I had wondered for some time what kind of woman it would take to pick his very unusual lock. Anyway, there she was. While knocking on doors somewhere with his new annuity plans, he had come across Miss Right.

Biggs was having a little difficulty getting the words out. His face radiated an expression of distant pleasure and said he had fallen in love with the way she laughed. In an almost misty way, he said that when she was laughing, the world seemed to brighten and pretty soon the years and his burdens would drop away. He would find himself laughing, too, feeling so light and happy he could fly.

I had never seen him like this. Dumfounded, I listened patiently, as he let on that if things kept on going as well as they had been with the annuity sales, I would meet her soon.

I told Biggs how good it made me feel to hear this and that it couldn't have happened to a nicer guy. Thanking him for confiding in me, I got up, and offered to have them over for dinner just as soon as he felt comfortable enough to call and take me up on my invitation.

Remembering that Ellen had made plans for later, I said good night. I walked toward the door with a warm sense of relief for old Biggsy feeling as though my quiet wish for his happiness had finally come to pass.

On the way back to Barstow in the twilight, I kept trying to guess what kind of lady old Biggsy had on the line. My relief for him didn't seem to slake my curiosity which, like an itch I couldn't reach, was tempting me to enlist Ellen's gossip networks; but naaa, nosing around in someone else's romantic affairs has just never been my style. Besides, I'd given him my word of honor." Lando took a long snort on his bottle of Corona, gasped with satisfaction, and continued.

"Didn't see Biggs again until March. That afternoon still hangs with me as if it were yesterday. I had just finished up a report before press time when Sean Mauldin, a buddy of mine from county sheriff's department, was on the phone. He said he was out in the hills east of Yermo with a rather unusual situation.

He said he would rather give me the scoop on this one. I pumped him for details but he refused and told me it would be best if I saw this situation for myself. He told me where to meet him, and I said I would be there as soon as possible.

Can't recall when I've ever been more curious about a call in my entire career. Drove about four miles east of town on the main highway and then turned north on an old paved road that went up into the foothills, all the while wondering what the heck was going on.

As I rounded a curve, there was Biggs's old Plymouth facing me, parked on the left side of the road just beyond a small bridge. About a quarter mile ahead, two cop cars were parked off on the right shoulder. Across from the cars there was an almost-new mobile home, nestled in a small grove of tamarisk trees.

I pulled in behind the first cop car, got out and went looking for Mauldin. He was filling out a report on his clipboard, sitting in a lawn chair under the trees beside the mobile home. He waved to me. I walked over and asked what had happened. He told me that the widow who owned this place, a Mrs. Downy, was a local elementary school teacher. She hadn't shown up for class that morning.

When the school office called her home, there was no answer. Fearing that something might have happened to their beloved third-grade teacher, the principal's secretary asked the sheriff's department to drop by and see if she was at home. Mauldin and his partner, another officer by the name of Evans, were dispatched. They had been at the mobile home for most of forty-five minutes. The county coroner's office had been informed, but both officers were pretty sure it was a heart attack.

I asked Mauldin why Herbert Biggs's old Plymouth was parked down the road. He told me with a wry curl on his lips that he rather expected that that was Herbie's best shot at discretion. He told me that I really ought to go have a look for myself.

Feeling like a rookie in a detective movie, I opened the aluminum screen door and went into a slightly cluttered living room. Officer Evans was sitting on the couch using the phone. I went through the kitchen, with a few dirty dishes from the night before still in the sink, down the hall past the partly sorted laundry in the bathroom, and opened the door to the master bedroom. It was obvious why Mauldin had been so tight-lipped.

There was a double bed across the width of the room with a large built-in mirrored headboard on the side wall. Biggs lay, buck naked, with his hairy arms and boney legs splayed out. From the dried blood puddled on the pillow, it looked as though the back of his head had been banged on the edge of the headboard. His face and whole upper body was buried under an enormous sallow mountain of corpulent female flesh.

Mrs. Downy stared wide open-eyed into oblivion, with a sad catatonic smile. Her head was craned into the large rectangular mirror that was fixed to the wall at the head of the bed. Three long cracks spread out from the point where her head struck the glass. She looked to be in her late forties. She would've been a tall, handsome woman if she had been lean; but this lady had really gone out of her way at the dinner table.

I weigh about 195, maybe 200--tell you, Graham ol' buddy, this chick was at least one and a half of me. She could have weighed as much as 300 pounds. It didn't take a lot of detective work to figure out what happened.

Sometime during the previous evening, Biggs and his lover got playful and ended up in her bedroom. She probably wanted to ride the range like a cowgirl, and he certainly wouldn't mind the ride while watching her burlesque show.

Somewhere between her happy trails and his bump and grind, her overtaxed heart just gave up in all the excitement. At least 200 pounds of her upper body came crashing down on poor Biggs, banging his head on the headboard, and knocking him out. With her weight and all of that pillowy flesh it would have taken only a couple of minutes to asphyxiate him.

I just stood there stunned. A solid cloud of black irony hung over me. I looked down at Mrs. Downy's otherwise pleasant face and tried to imagine the way Biggs might have seen her when she was laughing--laughing all of his lonely burdens away and making him feel so light he could fly.

I had seen enough. Back outside, I thanked Mauldin for letting me in on it early. He said he wanted to see how a good news reporter like me would handle a real kinky scoop like this. I told him it was definitely a poser.

I drove back down to Biggsy's old car and took the photograph you saw. I wasn't sure why I was taking it. I didn't feel much like writing. Perhaps a picture of that old worn out '48, was the only thing left of Biggsy's life that a good journalist should take with him. Then the ambulance came flashing by as I stood there in the ditch thinking about it. I put my Speed Graphic back in the car and headed home."

Lando realized that his relleno had gotten cold as he was talking. He picked up his fork and began to dig in. Camp had finished his chimichanga and was drawing lines in the condensation on his glass of ice tea.

"Whoa!" he exclaimed, "what a story. If the syndicated press had got hold of that one, the whole nation would have gotten a bang out of it--excuse the pun. What did Mauldin think when he read the story?"

"I really don't know what he thought," Lando mused, staring through the tinted windows at people walking by outside in the bright sunlight. "My old buddy Sean Mauldin was transferred to Needles about a week later, and I sort'a lost track of him after that."

Lando slipped his fork under the last cool piece of relleno and put it in his mouth. He chewed it slowly for a moment, then chased it with another long snort of Corona.

"That story would have been the wildest piece of journalism I'd ever done, and you know I could have done it justice." He tipped his Corona all the way back and drained out the last of the suds.

"But then," he continued with a composed resignation in his voice, "you're the first person I've ever told this to."

He set the bottle down and dragged out a thin film of water on the formica, "Aaahh. Maybe ol' Biggsy shouldn't mind my going back on my word of honor though.

Hell! It's been twenty years."

Walden's Ridge, Tennessee, 1995

Some with Strong Backs Waining Notes

Recently, in the wake of musing about natural history, philosophy, and agriculture, I began writing *poetic text* for a relief etching that I had completed in 1979. As I worked on the phrasing, my compassionate concern for one of humanity's most empowering and fundamental motivations began to surface.

In this literate image, a farm wagon becomes my metaphor for humanity. Farm wagons carry what is to be planted, tend the growing, and then bear the harvest. We as humans also carry what is to be planted, tend to our growing, and, in our several respective ways, bear the harvest of our planted choices.

In farming, what, when, where, and how much we plant seems to be a matter of our conscious choosing. In the flow of generations, however, our choices have a constant uphill struggle with formidable instincts. This struggle demonstrates that in our physical bodies, we are not separate and unique from, but primally linked to, every other life form.

The power of instinctive sexuality is so strong among all animals that it affects almost every aspect of their lives from puberty to menses. It is the nature of bisexual creatures that normal females come into some form of estrus, and normal males go through some kind of rut. The universality of this behavior makes the conclusion very hard to escape that there exists a DNA-based, life-force instinct very close to our will to live, which cares almost nothing about the quality of an individual's life beyond its genetic function to create the next generation.

This conclusion, if true, would tend to define a successful generation as one that survives until the babies can take care of themselves. All virtue, pleasure, or even maturity beyond that very basic biologic necessity would be simply gratuitous icing. The very meaning of life itself could be reduced to productive sex and nurturing. By stating this succinctly, I do not wish to minimize either of these crucial functions.

We humans have accepted a sort of ruthless commercial expedient for many lower life forms. We severely exploit some species by selectively breeding them, then we mass produce them for food or other human desires. Although most "21st Century Moderns" have the civility to sense moral outrage when even rumors of this kind of expedient thinking are applied to the final value of contemporary humans, our history is replete with similar breakdowns in our own humaneness toward one another.

Surely we humans are more than just DNA couriers. Why would we have labored so hard beyond our primitive origins, actively stabilizing a food supply, securing shelter, developing culture and civilization, if finally all that mattered was productive copulation and care of offspring? And yet, when it comes to answering the great ontological question of origins (Who are we?), DNA couriers seems to be the answer empirical science gives us.

As our ancestors gained a greater awareness of life, they also began to apprehend its unavoidable end. Ideas and myths about what happens to us after death evolved along with local wisdom over the centuries to form the world's great religions. One thing many religions have in common is that they promise a spiritual meaning beyond the temporal by linking their adherents through ritual and community to a deity or power that can transcend the opaque barrier of death. The desire to go beyond this barrier is almost a touchstone of consciousness in our development as a species.

But until someone actually demonstrates to all of humanity at the same time that our cognition can transcend death, we are left with the minimal chagrin of being highly evolved DNA couriers, who, because of our sentient powers, are faced with the responsibility of coming to a lasting, peaceful balance with each other and all the forms of life on this Earth. If we fail at that task, then we shall have been, in spite of the cornucopia of our otherwise awesome achievements, like a deadly bacteria whose crowning overpopulation caused the needless extinction of many other harmless forms of life. Sex and procreation are moving experiences. For most of us, these two experiences are the highest events in our lives. Unfortunately, we humans are far too numerous and wasteful to continue multiplying at the level of our instincts.

Scientists have determined that the Earth can comfortably sustain about two billion humans. At this writing, there are over six billion and by the year 2050 perhaps twice that number. Over half the Earth's human population currently lives below what we in America consider the poverty line. Because of our self awareness, we humans will ruthlessly defend our right to live, even to the point of destroying other species. All the great land and sea animals that live on the Earth with us are at the mercy of our instincts and intellect.

Solutions to the growing dilemma of our overly successful procreation will be worked out sooner, by a peaceful and humane all-world consensus, or later, by vicious and devastating conflicts over continuously shrinking resources amid mass extinctions and intolerable pollution.

If we can comprehend the cumulative effects of our forebearers' passions, paradigms, and prodigal dreams, then we also, like the son orphaned in the *poetic text* to this image, will keenly sense our need for greater understanding.

Were humanity to find that wise consensus of population control and put it into equitable use in time, it would be the most momentous event in the twenty-first century. It remains to be seen if we humans have the corporeal determination that it will take to evolve our own nature.

There are enough current examples of the misery and destruction overpopulation causes to make our options clear. We will either take the hard road of thoughtful change and peacefully work together toward the goal of a sustainable Eden, or continue to mindlessly cruise on down the super highway of our instincts to Hell.

Image size: 17" X 23" Edition of 50 impressions plus 15 proofs, hand-pulled by the artist, on 22" X 30" paper stock, some on Arches Buff and some BFK Rives.
Curation completed, June 1979. Plate canceled, January 1980.

Some with Strong Backs Waining

Eyes,
opening as in joy
or birth,
lashes,
lifting like a feathered mist
from freshly harvested fields
into clear twilight--
these
were the only jewels
he would take with him.

Through trials
and exhaustion,
and all of the pre-dawn hours
still sprinkled with stars
into which
waking,
he would begin
yet another day.
Her eyes remained
his only talisman.

Her eyes,
like unsullied pools
from a highland spring,
which in reflection
know stories
only the sky can tell,
reading the way of clouds
as they grow and wane,
turning in cycles
through the firmament,
offered his eyes
in that moment
enough
of forever
to last them both
a lifetime.

Lying back
among the soft
dappled sounds
of breeze
and stream,
they could see
the sun quartered late
beyond the tree line.
They could hear the team of greys,
ripping up mouthsful
of new grass as they grazed
still harnessed
to the wagon.
They could feel the crushing
spring carpet of dancing light
and green
transport them,
hold them,
pillow
their impassioned movements.

His young, hardened
plowman's hands
gently furrowed
her cashmere skin--
his fingertips describing
in the ecstatic words
of touch,
as only touch can,
the responsive rise and fall
of her virgin plains,
the resilient firmness
of her full hills
over whose soft
but turgid crests
his welcome fingers
danced and lingered
until the ache was keen.

RELIEF ETCHING
ARTIST'S PROOF
MALCOLM G. CHILDERS

Then
arching over,
his amber locks spilling down
with the kiss,
the flow
of his trembling touch
gathered
and like a flushed
and chilling wave
ran headlong in search
of the fountain of youth
hidden deep within
the tropic recesses
of her secret forest.

Her gasping,
grasping
fingers
splayed across his crown
pulling his locks down
to taste
her waters of life,
easily overpowered
his strong back
as she rose
to harmonize with him
in the yet unsung air
of their own
re-creation.

As heartbeats
drummed in their ears
over the rush
of urgent breathing,
all that he had grown to be,
all that he might ever be,
slipped
through her flowering
garden gate
into the transcendent warmth
of heaven.

Yes,
he could feel her deepest longing.
Yes,
she would take all of him.
Yes,
he could hold back nothing.
Yes,
she would be his bliss.
Oh yes,
they would give all
together.

Their eyes welled with emotion,
for the knowing
overflowed with joy,
for the giving
flooded with tears,
for the sweet soft
tangerine pain
of love.

Clinging to each other
until the sound
of the stream returned,
then
lying side by side,
they drifted
like sojourning flower petals
on the surface eddies of the river
into a deep, deep peace.

It was the waning light
through stout oaken spokes,
now too spent to defend
against the growing
chill of evening,
which brought them
out of their primeval slumber.
They hurried to dress--
she had to be elsewhere;
he would catch it for sure.

They would meet again
and again and again.
He, in the wagon
moving slowly down the river road;
she,
holding up her gingham dress,
hopping from stone to stone,
hoping he would wait,
hoping that
she would not be late.

One June afternoon
she confessed to him
how late she was,
with tears
and fear
in her beautiful eyes
cast down as in shame,
but he
would have none of it.

Laughing,
he wondered
if she
could long be happy
with only the love
of a common
working man.
She wiped her reddened eyes
and smiling,
wondered how
his common love
could so completely fill
her thoughts
and waking dreams.

He would work harder.
She would scrimp and save.
He would buy
the team and wagon.
She would gather her things.

They would marry
and
drifting like the summer dust
rising from the turn
of stout oak wheels,
settle in somewhere
afield,
camping at first,
then claiming,
clearing,
plowing,
planting,
building,
weeding,
harvesting,
storing,
weathering,

birthing.

So hard
for ones so young;
the nearest neighbors
came urgently,
under the thumbnail
of a quarter moon,
five miles at twilight
along rime-brittle fields,
hands
clutching hoods
in thick mittens,
reddened
from the biting wind.
The older woman
would do what she could,
having watched
her grandmother
pull three younger brothers,
red and wrinkled,
crying
into light of day.

The balding man
with simple,
honest eyes,
would help split more wood
to keep the snow,
shoveled from the roof,
boiling.
They brought with them
old sheets,
carbolic acid,
and a small sugar bag
filled with salt.

It was,
as he would recall later,
looking
with wavering voice
into his son's questioning eyes,
the worst and best night
of his life.
He looked down at fear and pain
in the eyes of his beloved,
wiped the sweat
from her flushed brow,
and gently told her
that she would be all right
in the face
of some deeper
unspoken dread.

The man child,
born of her final labor,
was blessed with her eyes.
Though he knew only
his father's arms,
(had her kindly disposition),
and though he tasted only
the milk of goats and cows,
grew up strong
with his father's back
for hard work.

The father
had little to give his son
beyond what the land could:
what he had learned
at his own father's side,
bittersweet memories of his wife,
how to build a house,
how to work a field.

Once on a trip
beside a grassy river bank,
the father talked long about
the all-consuming power of love
and the wonder of
their secret meetings.
Then,
almost as a confession,
he revealed his prodigal dreams
like indelible regrets,
wishing he had seen other places
and learned more about life,
wishing he
had somehow gone to school
(learned to read),
wishing
they had waited.

Their seventeenth year
on the place
needed a well
that would last through
the summer's
withering dry.
Standing waist deep
in the murky hole
one brisk morning
just before planting time,
slogging buckets
of mud
up to his son's
windlass turning,

the father pushed
his strong back,
as was his way,
and came up at midday
chilled to the bone.

Whether it was consumption
or pneumonia,
the son never knew.
A fever came on hard
at twilight
and with only a few words
from his father's pale lips
about looking
into beautiful eyes
along a green river bank,
it passed,
taking with it
the light from his eyes.
Only an expression
of deep peace remained
on his sallow countenance.

The grieving son
took what he could get
for the land of his childhood,
when he passed
through the commerce
of the nearest town.
The tired old wagon
carried a crude pine box
and little else to comfort him
as he moved slowly
down the river road.

Stopping
near a budding bower,
he fetched a worn shovel
from under the weathered seat
and planted the seeds
of his own beginnings
deep
in the emerging green.

He drove
the waining wagon
over the freshly
turned earth.

There
he unhitched the team,
locked the brakes down,
and left it to stand
for reasons
so deep
that the words
had not yet been born
in his mind
to think them.

Packing all he owned
on one horse,
he saddled the other
and rode away,
bearing the burden
of his father's
prodigal dreams,
keenly hoping
that he might
find someone
who could
"learn" him

how to read.

Walden's Ridge, Tennessee, 1995

A Prophet in Oxide Notes

I once asked Barry Parker, a writer friend, what he would do if his time were his own. He thought a while and said that his first project would be to write definitively about the big four and then see what inspired him after that. I asked who the big four were. He said, "You know, God, love, sex, and death." I admired his thought-provoking reply and remembered it when I was writing the text for this image.

GOD

I have never been able to think of or talk about God in other than abstract, subjective terms, even though any transcendent personality capable of creating the cosmos would certainly deserve the most honored status of consummate objectivity and reverence. Lacking the one-on-one global press-conference interview that would give us the sought-after jewel of provable extrinsic evidence, I will take the liberty of pretending that God's personal experience of us might be similar to the benevolent disembodied consciousness of the narrator for this image.

LOVE

Most romantic love comes to us in a rush of emotions as we let go of our ego boundaries. Blessed and happy are those who, after the gold rush is over, find that there are other reasons for staying on and making their lives work together. In fact, true love is often better defined by what happens after the gold rush is over, than any number of heartfelt vows during the heights of passion. There is a deeply fulfilling purpose in making love last, although quite often the effort may make you feel like a farmer. You will, occasionally, have to lie on your back in the dirt under your old truck of choice and chance with crank-case oil dripping down in your face, replacing those worn out rod and main bearings, just to keep it going.

SEX

Sex is both an elixir and an addictive drug. When we become involved, it is as though we had passed through a door that forever alters both the landscape and our purpose. Before we go through that door, most of us have a strong unfulfilled longing. On the other side, we have a hunger that needs satisfaction. How wisely we feed our new hunger can change our lives into anything ranging from a prosperous and beautiful countryside, to a blasted and howling wasteland. Unfortunately, this kind of wisdom comes to us, if ever, some years after we have taken our lives through that one-way door.

DEATH

Death, like the Latin words *terra incognita* on an old nautical chart, is the final mystery. Do we, as human beings, have a transcendent spiritual advantage over the rest of the animal kingdom with whom we share pain, death, and the dissolution and desiccation that follow?

In the hereafter, do we cycle through many changes of form as part of a learning process that will eventually allow us to achieve perfect unity with the impersonal cosmos?

Is our unique persona held in the mind of an omniscient being, capable of remaking us down to the molecule from memory, long after our bodies have turned to dust?

Will our choices and/or the moral quality of our lives determine whether we spend the rest of eternity in the depths of unspeakable torture or in the heights of transcendent bliss?

Will there be a final cosmic judgment where all the evils, injustices and disasters within the entire scope of human experience are given absolute resolution? Will we as conscious resurrected souls finally be given an infinite reason for our finite lives?

Is there a spiritual way of escaping the grip of creeping entropy. Or is time, that cosmic force we run our workday lives on, the one that takes our youth, our eyesight, our hair, our strength, our lives, and finally any memory that we ever existed, the final arbiter of eternity?

Does death feel like the leaden weight of an old truck being lifted from our bodies. Is it like taking off our boots in a mudroom, opening a door, and having someone whose love has changed us, ask on the eve of a long-awaited supper, what took us so long to come inside?

Image size: 15 1/2" X 22 7/8" Edition of 50 impressions plus 15 proofs, hand-pulled by the artist, on 22" X 30" paper stock, some on Arches Buff, some BFK Rives.
Curation completed, June 1979. Plate canceled, June 1979.

A Prophet in Oxide

May 28, 1977   10:27 a.m.

Immutable from dawn to dusk,
the remaining headlight
like a glass eye
glints in the sunlight
as if comprehending something
in the reedy gossip of wild oats.
The untamed margin grasses
rub their whiskered heads
against a crazed and colorful skin,
buffing arcs through oxides
of paint and steel as they
bow and sweep
in the cool morning breeze.

Through splayed open doors
creaking stiff on rusted hinges,
bunches of wheat grass reach
sinuous green fingers up
out of holes in the rotting
seat cushion fabric.
A flank of green blades
like spring on parade grows
in the thin layer of humus
atop the seat back.
The blades riffle in the wind,
which
has come to them across a sea
of waving grain
and in
through the broken rear window
of the cab.

October 22, 1971   6:17 p.m.

Tired and tread bare,
worn out rod bearings
rumbling on the crankshaft journals,
acrid blowby coming up
through the floorboards,
steam rising from the radiator,
he crunched the transmission
into reverse
for the last time
and backed the old flatbed off
into the weeds beyond
the equipment shed.
Killing the ignition,
he opened the door
and stepped out--
the autumn grasses complaining like
so many thin,
brittle voices.

Removing his sweat-stained straw hat,
he fanned the noxious blowby
away from his face
and felt the cool puffs of air
on his bald head.
An expression of peaceful resignation
crossed his countenance
as he surveyed the fields,
which now more than ever,
he thought of passing on
to his children.

Stretching out his arms like Jesus,
he willed with all his heart
that the land
would continue her bounty.

He leaned his head back
and shouted exuberantly,
"LET THERE BE LIFE,"
thinking that God might like to hear
an echo from Creation.

The radiator gurgled
and hissed a snarl of rusty water out
from under the cap.
He laughed
and,
in an almost reverent way,
slowly closed the door
until he heard the latch snap into place.
Wasn't this ratty old interior
once a nest of boundless passion?
Resting his arms
on the open window frame,
his thoughts seemed to spill backwards,
into a dreamy mist
from another autumn afternoon
forty years now gone.

October 19, 1931 4:37 p.m.

The new truck skin hissed
and beaded in the light rain.
A fog slowly closed in
on the small clump of trees,
behind which he had parked,
to be out of mind for a while.
It did not bother him knowing
that the affectionate young lady
sitting on his lap
had been in other laps
before his.
For some reason she
had taken to his shy,
awkward frame.
As he held her close,
his vision went dizzy with excitement.
His mind, his eyes seemed on fire.
His trembling hands fumbled
with the clasps on her halter.
His dry voice gasped with delight
at the beauty his hands
had just set free.
Her soft hands that had been
toying in his red curls
and caressing his neck,
now cradled his head
and gently drew him into the valley
of her shadow of life.
A place he confessed, smiling
to himself, that he never wished
to leave and so,
returned there often.

So often, in fact, that his father
gave him the truck and
a quarter section of land
to raise their children--all shy,
bright-eyed like their mother
and red-haired like their father.
"Like me," he smiled, "her and me."

His head bowed as if in prayer,
recalling what the minister had read
just before their marriage vows--
something about how a good woman
was of greater value
than silver and gold--
worth more than rubies and emeralds.
He saw the gold in her hair
as it swirled above him,
and her warm round dollars
describing arcs,
gracefully exaggerated by

the movement of her hips.
There she filled him with feelings
of warmth and love
that he would have given
his life to secure.
He saw her soft red mouth
lose its playful grin and
as if in pain or angelic delight,
moan, "Oh Caleb,
Oh yes, darling, Ohhhhh."
He saw the glow of love in the full flush
of her striking green eyes.

October 22, 1971 7:05 p.m.

"Greater than rubies and emeralds,"
he whispered.

Stepping back from the truck,
he thought of all the
harvest-time breakdowns,
the flat tires,
the hot afternoons until dark
spent
bending over those fenders
or sliding around on his back
in the dirt beneath it
replacing bearings,
trying to nurse
a few more thousand out of it,
trying to keep it moving,
trying to make a living for himself,
his children and his sweet
earthy treasure.

A giddy feeling like freedom,
like the weight of an old junker
seemed to lift from his body,
and
thinking how often
love had saved him,
he said to the truck,
"You an I, we've wrestled a bit.
There've been times I wished
I'd sold ya for scrap years ago--
damn if you couldn't be a pain
in the butt;
all too often when I needed ya most.
Well, anyway,
this here spot is yours
'cause I ain't forgot
there was a lotta good times, too.
I hope. . . this makes us even,
old timer."

Turning, he walked back
to the farmhouse
as the sun was slipping
into the long rolling tree line
on the hills across the valley.
He climbed the stairs
and pulled off his boots
in the mud room.
Turning the doorknob,
he went into the kitchen
and just caught the twinkle
in his wife's emerald eyes.

"So, my daddy beau,
what took ya so long
out beyond the shed, hmmm?"
she winked, with a half-peeled potato
in her wet hands.
"Rites and blessings, my love,"
he said lifting a lid on the stove.
"What's fer supper?"

Walden's Ridge, Tennessee, 1995

Front Range Gold Notes

Ever since man first discovered the useful properties of metal, beginning with copper some 6500 years ago, mining the Earth has been a signal event in the growth of civilization. One of the earliest sites of mining and smelting lies near the town of Bor in the former Yugoslavia. The mining sites were found by archeologists studying the Vinca culture's development of coppersmithing and its earliest proliferations before the Bronze Age. The sites they studied were barely discernible scars in a cliff face.

The metal concentration in the ore at these early Balkan mines had to be very high to justify the grueling hand labor. Back then, ore had to be broken free from the deposit with either stone hammers, antler picks, or a technique called fire quenching. This last method involved heating the working face with wood fires, then quenching the hot rocks with water using thermal contraction to crack ore off the deposit. They obviously used wood fires to smelt the metal out of the ore, but exactly how these early metalsmiths, with their rudimentary technology, were able to smelt the great volume of ore they did is still a mystery in search of an answer.

Early metal workers had little chemistry with which to develop the Bronze Age. Today, modern chemistry and applied technology allow us to pursue profitably very low concentrations of metal in the ore deposits we find. The downside of these advances is that many of these modern processes require deadly poisons like cyanide and mercury to dissolve and capture the metal. The use of such toxins can easily destroy the natural integrity of the mine and mill site, not to mention ecosystems downstream and those within adjacent wind patterns.

For only an ounce of precious metal, we often disrupt tons of earth with our heavy mining equipment, disturbing and polluting aquifers which, in turn, affect other economies. When maximizing profit becomes the only mandate of a resource company, how a site is treated is of minimal concern, and the scars left on the land have a way of becoming far more draconian than benign points of archeological interest.

Early in the last century, many mining and milling concerns possessed the dangerous know-how of production before they became aware of the long-term environmental effects of their technology. While it may not seem fair to hold those who did their damage in ignorance to the same standards we expect of contemporary companies, the burden of cleaning up these older poisoned environments still falls largely on those who have had nothing to do with, and very little benefit from, the industry. This situation is a contemporary burden that all of us must bear.

It would be nice to believe that corporations with their wealth, their intimate know-how, and a public image to maintain would be their own best watchdogs, and that government regulations would be like backyard fences between good neighbors. However, the fact that our government has had to create such a thing as an environmental cleanup Superfund is prior evidence of the public distress caused by the private sector's failure to self-regulate. Given all that we currently know about our ecology, when a contemporary resource company dodges its environmental responsibility, the act is hard to read as other than a willful exploitation of the public trust for private gain.

Whenever cases of such exploitation crop up, whether legally sanctioned or not, those involved are taking a shameful destructive advantage of responsible autonomy, a central ethic, and a principal privilege of the free enterprise system.

Rather than an invective against mining, I wanted this image with its words to function more like an archival movie. Single words and short phrases in the *poetic text* were intended to flicker past the reader's consciousness in much the same way we experience a silent film. I wanted the image and words to generate a kind of moving historical drama about one mine site in Colorado from its origin as a prospector's strike down through time to its present ruin.

Such ruins are often intriguing examples of the lengths to which we have gone, in an effort to produce portable, tangible wealth. Because of their historic significance, many of these old diggings and their structures possess a compelling romantic quality.

And yet, when I think of the massive open-cast operations that move and crush millions of cubic yards of very low-grade ore, then spread it on leach fields and treat it with cyanide so that minute amounts of gold can be recovered, my notions of historic romance evaporate along with any sense of reasonable propriety.

During the years I was creating the etchings in this book, I worked out a new definition for the word "rich." Although it doesn't address mining specifically, my hypothesis does deal with one of the central reasons humans have, over the centuries, mined the Earth's crust for minerals. My definitive hypothesis is this:

The most valuable thing we will ever personally own is our experience of this living planet within the Cosmos. The larger that experience is, the richer we are, even if we can sustain only our daily needs. If, however, that experience remains small, we are poor, though we dwell as kings.

Image size: 15 3/8" X 19 1/4" Edition of 260 impressions plus 42 proofs, hand-pulled by the artist, on 20" X 26" Arjomari paper stock (173 numbered impressions on Arches Cover, 10 numbered impressions on Arches Text, 30 numbered impressions on Rives lightweight, 14 on BFK, and 33 numbered impressions on Arches Light). Curation completed, October 1991. Plate canceled, August 1988.

Front Range Gold

divide
thin air
tundra zone
snow melt
cold
sweet water ponds
domain of clouds

eagles
hawks
owls
pikas
hares
marmots
whitetail
bighorn
mountain goat
elk
grizzly bear

short grass
alpine flowers
small shrubs
couched
on a rich
mineral
outcrop
decomposing

prospector
pack mules
picking
shoveling
sweating
panning
discovering
dancing

assays
claims
entrepreneurs
speculating
negotiating
investing
lawyers
contracts

overseers
engineers
roads
teamsters
horses
wagons
equipment

logging
carpenters
tents
kitchens
outhouse
boarding house
office

miners
worksite
blasting
overburden
track
ore cars
rock dumps

blasting
tunneling
shoring
mucking
ore veins
mine head
lift room
steam hoist
assay room
machine shop
magazine

blasting
drifts
stopes
pockets
raises
vents
shoring
track

blasting
high grade ore
pilfering
mucking
hauling
excitement

rattle
of tipple
rumble
of jaw crushers
thunder
of stamp mills
din
of shaker tables
ribbons
of gold
silver
copper
and lead

recapturing
processes
mercury
cyanide
slurry pipes
wooden dams
settling ponds
tailings
leaching

"FRONT RANGE GOLD"
RELIEF ETCHING
ARTIST'S PROOF
1 JUNE, 1986
MALCOLM G. CHILVERS

assay tickets
balance sheets
profits
dividends
industrial
and
corporate pride

blasting
ground water
pumps
pipes
roof falls
shoring
cave ins
casualties
dissatisfaction
safety and wage
disputes
unions
strikes
violence
federal restraint
arbitration
reconciliation

blasting
assay tickets
low grade ore
price falls

cut backs

layoffs

balance sheets

losses

closings

good-byes

abandonment

silence

heavy winters
deep snow
ice formation
unbearable weight
structural collapsing
spring thaws
tailing pond floods
dam failure
erosion
leaching
pollution

summer thunder
heavy rains
tailing erosion
spawning ground
silting
leaching
pollution.

Autumn colors

and visitors
from
a future time

stand
on the present site
of this
industrial expedient,

wondering
if indeed

everything

was considered
on the
balance sheets.

Alta, Colorado, 1986

Lockheed Lodestar Notes

Whenever there was a vacation of sufficient length in my college teaching schedule, I would load my van and go for a ramble. These trips were usually sort of destination-free and yet purposeful travel. Late in the spring of 1975, I went rambling West from my home in Tennessee on one such adventure.

For several days I had been photographing possible drawing subjects in small towns on the Colorado Plains. Looking at the map, I saw how close I was to Boulder. I decided to call friends who lived just east of town. They invited me to a party they were having that afternoon.

On the way to their house, I passed the airport where this vintage airplane caught my attention. After taking a few pictures, I went on to the party where I mentioned what I had just seen. My friends passed on local gossip about the plane as we reminisced, crunching on chips and dip under the cottonwoods shading their backyard.

After I returned home and developed my film, the old airplane continued to captivate me. I finally chose it as a subject because I liked the sweeping form of the airplane fuselage and its visual interaction with the sky. When the drawing was done, it occurred to me that in spite of the friendly backyard gossip, I still knew very little about the actual events surrounding this aircraft.

Lacking the time and resources for research, I decided to begin with what I knew and fill in the blanks with invented narrative. That might at least add a kind of virtual depth to my experience. The short story I wrote extrapolates the local gossip my friends told me into a plausible, if not dramatic, account.

While I was still in the flush of completing the text to this piece, I became impressed with the creative potential of fiction to influence personal perspectives. I thought of the many times history has been shaped by great works of fiction.

Then it occurred to me how many times we humans have created fiction that eventually became significant world views. Based on little more than the hearsay I used to generate my story, other fictions have become the rallying cry for brutal human conflict and devastation.

Finally, I was left in a blue funk, trying to think of one war that didn't fit this disturbing scenario.

Image size: 17 3/8" X 22 3/4" Edition of 50 impressions plus 15 proofs, hand-pulled by the artist, on 22" x 30" paper stock; some on Arches Buff, some on BFK Rives.

Curation completed, January 1982. Plate canceled, January 1982.

Lockheed Lodestar

Gerald 'Spud' Jeffers gradually felt his butt go numb. He marked his place in the murky detective novel with the stub from his last paycheck and set the dog-eared paperback on a small filing cabinet. Draining his coffee, he stretched his arms, and got up out of the army-surplus office chair.

Slipping a security-band radio onto his belt, he picked up his lunch box and opened the door. The moonlit tarmac with its apron of neatly parked private planes stretched away from the small guard building.

It was an almost perfect evening along the Front Range, with the Rockies looming up as gray silhouettes in the west. He walked over to the open window of the guard van and set his lunch box on the passenger seat. The moon was so bright he could easily read his watch. It was 2:44 a.m. when he started his round. He started this one a little early so he could have more time later to eat "lunch" on the small hill across the runway.

"The bivouac," as he called it, gave him a commanding view of the whole airport out to the ends of the runway. Since there was very little air traffic on the graveyard shift, he could eat his lunch and listen to his favorite late night program on the van's FM radio without noisy interruptions.

He would muse about things he hoped to do, girlfriends, and good times as he walked between the security clocks, checking doors and offices. *Sorta' greases up the hours,* he thought, as he returned and punched in.

Locking the guard shack door, he drove the van up to his night "lunch" bivouac. He switched off the ignition, set the parking brake, and reached over to turn on the radio. The jazz bridge in "Light My Fire" spilled into the night. Smiling, he ran his stout fingers through his thinning salt-and-pepper hair.

Picking up his lunch and opening the door, he stepped out on the short grass and did a little foot-boogie to the driving beat as he went around the vehicle. Sliding open the side door, he sat down on the floor of the van with his feet on the ground and opened his lunch box. Taking out a salami on rye, he thought, *Heck, apart from staying alert and checking the stations every hour, all I gotta do right now is enjoy this humble repast.*

"Not bad," he toasted with a smile, lifting his salami on rye as if it were a shot glass, then taking a big bite. *Hell,* the stray thought caught him off guard, *I know what bad is.*

His smile melted away like a snowflake on a warm exhaust pipe. A sickly, nauseating chill passed through him like shadows across the moon. He tried to shake it off, but he was there again on that night of January 31, 1968. He could feel the humidity, the weight of the M-16 in his sweating hands. He and his good friend Franklin Jamar Fontain, a beefy oil rig worker from Plaquemines Parish, Louisiana, were guarding a row of helicopters at the Air Base in Da Nang.

"I'm wondering, Frankie," he was asking again quietly, "are nights in Viet Nam anything like nights in Louisiana?"

"Aw man, no way. Nighs back home is fill wi flowers an luv an happy foks. Dis place got sum kina ba shi ju ju. Ever sinh I got here, its lie someone outdair jus waytin fa me ta turn ma back. Is sorta lie the devil you can't see is da wan who getsta blow you away. An Charlee, he got all deez ways a bein dair even

wen you don know he is. Only peace I got is dat I'ma short timer here. Ten mo an a wakeup baby, an my young aaz iz flien outta here on one'na dem big ramp butt freedom birds. Thank ya Jeasus an gud riddenz."

The two of them had just turned to work their way back down the line of choppers when Franklin's German Shepherd lunged forward, yanking on its leash and barking at something in the dark beyond their perimeter.

The dog yanked him between a sniper and Spud. A bullet caught Franklin and knocked him flat backwards off his feet. Franklin's shepherd bolted away, growling into the night. Shots from another position caught the dog. It tumbled over, rolling, jerking and yelping painfully in the dust.

Then, the whole night erupted with gunfire. Mortar rounds were coming in, flares were going up, and terror reigned. Spud dropped to the apron and rolled over to his friend. He ripped open Franklin's bloody fatigue shirt. It was obvious even from the light of flares and explosions that he had a sucking chest wound.

"You're gonna be all right, man," Spud said, fumbling with the compression bandage, cursing quietly, trying to get it fixed under the bloody shirt in a way that would allow him to be carried. Franklin lay there with a catatonic expression on his face, coughing blood.

And then he was staggering along, bent over, carrying Franklin's solid bulk on his back, gasping, yelling for help through the flashes of the death storm erupting all around them. Two of the choppers were hit. The burning magnesium clouded the night with a smoky glow that was stabbed by the staccato ratchet of popping machine gun shells.

By the time Spud got to the medics, he had been nicked in the leg and the arm. Franklin died an hour later on the operating table. The pitched battle lasted until dawn.

The morning after what he later learned was called the Tet Offensive, Spud saw the body bags from that one fire fight lined up in long rows as they were being loaded into a C-130. He couldn't help but wonder which one Franklin was in. The very thought of how close he had come to going home in a body bag like his friend had a devastating effect on his nerves. He was given a month's R and R after he got out of the Med. Evac. hospital.

When he reported back to duty, however, he suffered from repeated flashbacks of the nightmare he had witnessed. At times, his fear of death brought on crippling panic attacks. Desperate for some way to control fear's debilitating effects, he took to smoking hard Asian marijuana. He loathed the taste of the smoke, but it calmed him enough so that he could make it through the rest of his tour without losing control.

Spud could not forget what he had been through when he returned home, but he never felt a need for marijuana again. He let the weed with all of his painful memories slip behind him, like rice paddies in the window of the transport plane bound first to Saigon, then home.

Spud felt cold with sweat. It had happened again as it always did, without warning and always the same way. He would just snap and start vividly reliving that same night--that same scene of horror over and over.

As a civilian Spud would occasionally suffer post-traumatic stress episodes. While they were not enough to qualify him for disability, he knew that that bit of information on his medical records had significantly limited his range of occupations.

Spud stared out at stars along the horizon and then down at his trembling hands holding the remains of a tortured sandwich.

"Damn all wars forever," he said quietly.

Tears and sweat were running down his face.

Vaguely in the distance behind him and just over the bedroom voice of the DJ, he could hear the drone of a twin-engine plane. He finished his mangled sandwich and washed it down with sweet warm tea from his thermos, consoling himself with the thought that by some grace he had made it through and for him, war and drugs were part of a gruesome past he might someday forget. The drone of the airplane grew and changed pitch as though it were making an approach.

That's odd, he thought, *I haven't heard any landing requests on the airport band.* Spud got up and walked out in front of the van so he could view the whole runway. He was just in time to see an old Lockheed Lodestar settling in for a final approach with no landing lights.

"Je-sus, Mary and Jo-seph! What is he trying to do?" Spud erupted, running back, stuffing his lunch in the box and sliding the van door shut. When he got to the front of the van, he noticed that the Lodestar was coming in too high, as if the pilot couldn't see the runway very well and was hesitating to set it down. Spud scrambled into the driver's seat, started the van. He spun off down the hill onto the runway after the airplane.

The pilot had used up a lot of concrete being cautious, but he touched down on the last third of the strip. By the time he slowed enough to turn the plane, he was in the dirt, about two hundred feet beyond the runway.

The late '30's tail dragger was a sight to see, bumping around in the rough, stirring up a rooster tail of dust in its prop wash. Even in the moonlight Spud could see that someone had given the old plane an elegant new paint job.

The pilot was halfway through his turn when, all of a sudden, the starboard wheel dropped down about a foot. The pilot revved up the starboard engine, but the plane would not budge. He revved up both engines and fanned the rudder. Still nothing happened. He cut the engines, and the props coasted to a sputtering halt.

By the time Spud stopped the van in front of the Lodestar, the pilot had crawled out of the emergency hatch and stood on the wing, cussing a blue streak. Spud wiped his face on his sleeve, slipped out of the van, and went over to look at the half-buried wheel. It was soon obvious to him what had happened.

"Well," he said, looking out from under the wing, "that's one squashed prairie dog home!" Spud's humor had a calming effect on the pilot. He eased down to the trailing edge of the wing, jumped off into the dust and took a look for himself.

"Damn! If it ain't one thing, it's another. I must have a wiring problem. First my fuel gauge starts acting up, then my radio goes blinko. Then when I try to get it down, no landing lights, and now this. Oh, I'm sorry, forgetting my manners," the pilot said stretching out and shaking Spud's hand.

"Al Grasser's the name. Listen, if you can just get me to a phone, I got some friends in town with 4x4's and shovels. They can have me outta here in no time."

"Yeah, the airport manager will definitely want to have you out'ta the flight paths by sunup," Spud noted. "There's a phone you can use up in the lounge. I'll give you a lift."

As they drove back up the runway, Al went on about how he had spent most of his flying time in nose wheel aircraft, and he still wasn't used to tail draggers.

"The hardest part of landing the low wing jobs," he explained. "is that you can't tell where the damn runway is until yer grinding the skin off yer butt."

"I expect all that just takes a little gettin'

used to," Spud commented, as he opened his lunch box and started on his next sandwich. When they reached the hangar, he stopped outside of the lounge, got out and unlocked the door. "There's a phone and a john in here," he motioned to the pilot, flipping on the lounge lights. "Let me know how it goes with your friends. I'll be out here in the van."

"Hey, thanks," Al replied, walking toward the rest room. Spud went back out to the van and took a thoughtful drink from his thermos. Something was bothering him. Was it the fact that the pilot crawled out of the emergency hatch instead of the main entry door in the rear of the plane? Perhaps it was something in the pilot's eagerness to explain away the very unusual circumstances of this landing.

He looked back through the lit window. The pilot was still in the john. Spud reached into the van, turned the security radio on to low volume, flipped the switch to the local police band and got the mike off the dash. Pulling the coiled cord out of the window and around to the blind side, he keyed the mike and got the local dispatcher.

"Hey, Zack, Spud here, out at the airport. Listen man, I might need some very discrete help. We gotta big twin-engine airplane with one wheel stuck in a prairie dog hole at the east end of the runway. The pilot doesn't know I'm calling--'tell ya, there's something odd about this situation, man. Could be some kind of contraband. Could you send some cruisers and a plain Jane with her glasses on, out to the airport road neighborhood and stay out'ta sight. Your guys will see one or more 4x4's coming to pull the airplane out'ta the hole. I'm gon'na play dumb with the pilot. Stand by until I confirm the situation. Do you read me?"

The radio hissed a quiet affirmation. Spud keyed the mike again and said, "Don't do anything without my cue. Gotta go, bye,"

He had just turned off the radio and hung up the mike when he saw the pilot through the picture window. He had come out of the john, picked up the phone and dialed. Spud reached for his second sandwich, leaned back against the van and looked up at the full moon. He was just finishing his tea when Al came out of the lounge.

"Any luck?" Spud asked.

"Yeah, I got solid friends. They'll be out in about half hour, forty-five," he said, breathing deeply and stretching.

"You can wait here in the lounge till they show up, if you want," Spud suggested.

"Aah," the pilot wavered. "I guess I'll walk back and try to figure out how to get my plane out'ta this mess. Maybe the walk'll help."

"Suit yourself," Spud replied. "I'll open the main gate for your friends. Say, just for security purposes, how many and what kind of vehicles am I letting in here to help you?"

The pilot thought for a moment, rubbing the back of his neck. "There'll probably be a couple of pickups and a custom 4x4 van that one of my buddies put together himself."

"I've gotta ask this kind'a stuff 'cause it's my fanny on the line out here and being careful is what this job is all about," Spud explained in a conciliatory tone.

"Hey man, no problem. I understand," the pilot said, turning and walking back toward the ghostly form of the old transport.

As Spud parked the van on the far side of the guard shack, he noticed a white Ford sedan pull up under a cottonwood tree on the residential edge of the airport. The car's lights went out. He picked up the mike and flipped on the radio.

"That you in the plain white paper bag?" he asked, with his lips on the mike.

"Sounds like Idaho Red," the radio hissed.

"How much did ya bring for the party?" Spud asked.

"Gotta six pack," the radio hissed again.

"Good, this could be a kegger. I'm going to leave the front door open for our guests. You keep an eye on it for me, while I go upstairs and watch the program. I'll be there to give you sports fans instant coverage. It might be best, if this is the real thing, to let our guests get out the front door a half mile or so, before you check their pockets. There's a lot of ritzy hardware here, ya know. Key me twice if you copy." He let up on the send button and two clicks broke through the squelch.

Spud hung up the mike and reached for the big ring of keys in the glove compartment. He got out of the van and walked over to the sliding hurricane and barbed wire gate by the guard shack. He snapped open the padlock, but hesitated to shove the main entrance gate open, wondering if the limits of his personal discretion weren't being exceeded. Walking back to the van, he unzipped and took a pee in the dirt on the edge of the tarmac.

Spud found his binoculars in the top drawer of the guard shack filing cabinet. He had considered slipping up to his bivouac hill but reminded himself that it would appear more natural if he were to act the role of an unsuspecting guard and stay at the shack at least until the rescuers arrived. He realized he was putting himself at greater risk by showing his face, but it might look like a trap if the gate were open, and he wasn't around.

He didn't have to wait long. Within twenty minutes, a 4x4 Ford pickup with big mud grip tires, a Chevy Blazer, a GMC van, and a 4x4 Dodge van turned up the entrance road. Spud got up from the squeaky chair and stepped out to open the gate. His middle-aged heart was thumping like an irrigation pump, but he was determined that he would not show any apprehension. He rolled the gate open just as the high-wheeler Ford pulled up.

"We've come to get our buddy Al Grasser out'uva hole he's got himself into somewhere out here," the rough voice behind the glow of a cigarette said from the dark interior of the truck.

"Yeah, he's down at the east end of the runway. Just go straight past the hangar and hang a left. You'll see him down there," Spud directed, talking loud over the loping rumble of header pipes while keeping his own face in the shadow of the gate post as much as possible. "Oh, and work fast. The airport will need to have you guys out'ta here by sunup."

"Don't worry, guard man, we didn't exactly come to party, ya know," the voice replied with thinly veiled disrespect. The engine revved, and the truck passed on through the gate, leading the motley group of customized vehicles with it.

Spud got his binoculars from the guard shack and walked through the standing rows of aircraft. He slipped quickly across the runway to the far side of his bivouac hill, feeling almost confident that he had not been seen. He lay prone in the short grass, where not more than a hour before he had had one of his recurring traumatic episodes. He put the binoculars to his eyes, then focused on the vehicles and the vintage airplane at least two-thirds of a mile away.

The pickup and the Blazer had stationed themselves in front of the Lodestar's wheels. He could plainly see two of Al's friends busy digging a ramp in the dirt for the starboard wheel. Another pair were fixing nylon ropes from the landing gear axles to the bumper hitches on the two trucks. It was the activity around the two vans that intrigued Spud.

He shifted the binoculars and fine focused. The 4x4 Dodge van had pulled up by the rear entry of the airplane, and one of Al's friends had opened the hatch. The other van had backed up to the wing on the far side of the plane. Although the 4x4 van was higher than normal, Spud could still detect very vigorous activity between the airplane and the vans. Al's friends were busy unloading the Lodestar.

"Bingo," Spud chuckled. Rolling over on his side, he slipped the two-way out of his belt. He thumbed the send button and spoke.

"Looks like a real party, sports fans. Better check those ticket stubs for winning numbers as you leave the ball park this evening." He let up on the button and listened for some reply. In the pale pre-dawn light, he could see that they were about to free the Lodestar.

Within a few seconds, he heard his radio hiss. "Our courteous staff is waiting to serve you at the snack bar." Spud gave a sigh of relief as he turned his attention back to the binoculars, knowing that at least he wasn't going to have to perform the arrest.

It was becoming difficult in the growing glow of sunrise to see precisely what was happening, but he could see well enough to tell that the crew had pulled the airplane free and were in the process of roping the tail wheel assembly of the airplane to the bumper hitch of the big 4x4 Ford. They were moving it around so that it could be towed backwards up to the fueling apron next to the hangar.

The rest of Al's friends were coiling rope, shoving bags into the vans, and sliding side doors shut. It was past time for Spud to be all the way back across the runway appearing officially unaware. He retreated quickly across the flight line, nearly tripping on a wing tie-down, as he ran, weaving head-long, across the apron through the standing aircraft. He reached the shack and got inside. Spud slipped the binoculars back into the file cabinet and collapsed into his old office chair.

"I guess, ha ah. I'm too outta shape, ha ah, for this kinda crap," he gasped.

Through the half open window of the guard shack, Spud could hear the header pipes of the big Ford 4x4 over the faint din of the other three vehicles, as they pulled up on the far side of the hangar. He heard their engines drop to an idle while they stopped to untie the Lodestar.

It was five eternal minutes before they revved their engines and started around the corner of the hangar toward the entrance. Spud was thankful that he had not closed the gate. He was eager to be rid of them. As they approached, he smiled and waved them on through. When they had gone a safe distance down the entrance road, he reached over and flipped on the security band radio. "Let's check 'em for silverware, boys," he said, into the mike in a Bogartesque mumble.

The line of vehicles turned off the airport entrance road and had just started moving up the highway when one, two, three, four, five patrol cars and the one unmarked spotter slipped out of hiding along residential side streets and converged on the entourage with red lights flashing, blocking any escape.

Spud left his radio on so that he could hear what was shaping up out on the highway. It wasn't long before he heard a friendly voice in the speaker hissing, "Hey Spud, ol' buddy, the city law boys owe you a tall cold beer for this one. Whoah! There's enough grass here to cover all of our lawns including the mayor's, not to mention the seeds and stems. Excellent detective work, my man."

Spud was beginning to feel pretty clever about the night's escapade. Folding his arms with satisfaction, he leaned back in the chair and was about to put his feet up on the desk when a realization came up and mugged him from behind. Where was the pilot? If he wasn't with his busted friends, he might at that moment be in the Lodestar about to take off.

Spud reached for the mike. "Boys, I didn't see the pilot, Al Grasser, leave here. He's about six feet, 210, gray eyes, short light brown hair, and wearing a blue jumpsuit. If he isn't in your custody, then he is still up here. He may be planning to take off. If you don't have him, get me some help up here immediately. I've gotta go check this out."

Putting the mike back on its radio hook, he pulled his revolver and checked the cylinder, then ducked out of the guard shack and ran over to the hangar. He moved cautiously along the wall of the building until he came to the corner. With his gun hand high, he eased around to see if the pilot was on the flight line.

The Lodestar was standing on the fueling apron, facing directly away from him into the morning sun with its elevator flaps down. The rear entry door was open.

Spud subconsciously realized that he was at a significant disadvantage trying to see into the glare of sunrise. He thought he saw a small movement in the elevator flaps. He couldn't tell for sure if it was the wind or maybe the pilot inside preparing to take off.

Braking cover, Spud moved out around the tail section of the airplane toward the open door. Scanning the aircraft with his eyes and his gun arm straight out, he paid special attention to the dark opening in the fuselage where the pilot might be hiding.

If Spud was wondering why Al had not already taken off, it was very apparent now. The lock on the AV gas pump was broken, and the pilot had been refueling at airport expense. The hose had been quickly flung aside. There was a small puddle of fuel by the nozzle and the pump was still on.

"Freeze! You nosy bastard." The pilot's voice came from behind with a vindictive edge. "This would 'a been my last cash run. I coulda had my plane paid for, but you--you gotta start playing mister clever ass nark. Well, I'm flying it outta here, and I'll be hung-damned before I let some two-bit security guard tie my wings down."

It occurred to Spud that the flashing lights on the highway had tipped him off as he was fueling up. In a panic, he probably hid in the 18-inch recess of the big hangar door.

"If you take off now, you know the Feds'll just track you on radar. You're gonna get caught anyway. So why not save yourself a whole world of grief, and just give up now?"

"Right, and that's why you're coming with me just like an insurance policy. Now lose the gun and step over easy toward the plane!"

Spud sensed a nauseating helplessness. A gripping chill caused his flesh to crawl, his eyes to blur, and then he was bleeding again. Struggling to get his friend off the flight line--yelling for help over the waves of insane red rage. The explosions and gunfire flashing on Franklin's fading face seemed to pass right through him. He knew he would never make it if the bullets kept coming. He tried hard to focus, but his mind was like a cornered wild animal. This time he would have to fight back. The bullets kept on hitting all around him--close to him. There was no other choice. This time he would have to take out the sniper.

His hands were trembling as he stretched out and stooped over as if to set his revolver down. But then like a spring wound tight, he slipped over sideways into a fast left roll on the asphalt, bringing his gun arm around to bear on the voice behind him. He heard a shot mid-roll and felt a sharp painful tug in his thigh. A second shot snapped into the pavement by his ear, but it did not affect the force of his intention. He raised his 357 Magnum and fired directly into the blurry form of the pilot. The pilot jerked back, stumbled, and fell flat on his back, his head bouncing on the fueling pavement.

When the sound of the gas pump returned to Spud's consciousness, he set down his gun and looked at the prostrate pilot. He didn't hate this guy. He wasn't even angry enough to haul off and pop him hard for his snotty attitude. It began to dawn on him that this "bust" was uncomfortably like living out a scene in one of his detective novels.

A throbbing ache in his left thigh brought him back hard into his own situation. He was bleeding bad enough to know that he had to get a tourniquet on his leg quickly. Removing his belt, he wrapped it high near his crotch and pulled the leather as tight as he could before tying it off. He dragged himself over to the pilot, leaving a dark trail of his own blood on the tarmac.

The pilot was unconscious from the fall, but it was obvious to Spud as soon as he unzipped his jumpsuit that the bullet had punctured his lung. Spud, in his weakened state, could think of nothing to do for the pilot but pull off his gray guard shirt, roll it up like a compression bandage and hold it in place on top of the pilot with his own fainting body weight.

Three minutes later, the municipal police found them both in critical condition that way. In the ambulance, Spud, started talking earnestly under the wail of the siren. It was as if he were trying to console a good friend in spite of his own sweating, trembling delirium. The E.M.T. administering plasma leaned over to check his pulse and could just make out the words he was saying,

"It's OK, Frankie. I nailed that sneaky son-of-a-bitch. Nobody's gon'na be hiding in the dark, waiting to blow us away, brother. Don't gotta smoke that damn hemp shit no more, man. Not anymore.

War's over."

Some three weeks later, an artist wandering around the West saw the Lodestar from the highway. He drove his VW camper up the airport road, through the gate, over dark stains in front of the hangar, and down to where the airplane stood impounded on the grass beside the taxi ramp.

Say, this really is something, he thought, walking around the airplane, cradling a six-by-seven camera on his arm. *The fuselage has a flow almost like Brancusi's stone fish. Hey, check out the sliding arch of these lines and the wonderful interaction of the sky on the new paint job--love the stretching sweep of these wings. Damn if it doesn't look like she's flying, even with her wings tied down.*

Boulder County, Colorado, 1993

Relief Etching Imagery

A Historical Overview of the Artist's Technique

RELIEF PRINTING: Origins and Process

The genesis of everything we now call printing began well before the time of Christ. The earliest artifacts of this craft are seal stamps that were carved from stone, wood, or clay for use in trade and government.

Archeologists have turned up evidence of the early use of seal stamps in civilizations as diverse as Egypt, Babylon, Rome, and China. Seals not only bore the signet of authority on important documents in these ancient cultures, but they also were used to brand cattle with ownership and criminals with descriptions of their offense.

These early seal stamps worked on the simple but effective idea that a flat piece of tractable material could be carved into, leaving the desired image remaining on the virgin surface. The image could then be replicated in wax, clay, or other substances. This first invention in a chain of ideas led to the development of printing.

The second link was the Chinese invention of paper around 105 AD by Ts'ai-Lun, a court official during the reign of Emperor Hoti. Ts'ai-Lun experimented for 25 years before he succeeded. He was made a Marquis and then put under house arrest for life in the Imperial Palace to prevent the spread of his remarkable invention.

Initially paper provided a more convenient material on which to paint or write; however, it was its eventual use as a substrate for printing that gave this remarkable material its ability to change civilizations.

Some years later, an unknown Chinese genius took the new cellulose fiber substance, dampened it, and laid it on a pre-existing relief wall tile, then lightly brushed the damp paper until it conformed to the relief image on the tile. When he applied an ink cake to the now-raised paper surface, it picked up the previously carved image. This stone-rubbing sequence could be repeated over and over with similar results, making it the first printing process.

The next development in the craft was to apply ink directly to relief-carved wood blocks with brushes, rollers, or daubers. The Chinese found that it was easier to ink the woodblock surface first, then apply the paper and pressure to complete the image transfer. This refinement of the stone-rubbing idea was not only the origin of relief printing as a specific craft, but it was also the beginning of the very idea of printing that has grown to become, within the intervening two millennia, a fine-art medium as well as a multi-billion-dollar commercial industry.

Buddhism valued both words and pictures for doctrinal teaching in its sacred texts or sutras. This religious application gave the new craft an external impetus for technical improvement.

The process of relief woodblock printing proliferated throughout the Oriental world and had a thousand years to develop in the hands of its artisans before it was brought to Europe by traders. A French woodcut dated 1380 is the oldest known example of the process in Western Civilization.

Today we still use this earliest of printing methods in processes such as rubber stamps, in all material forms of block printmaking, wood engraving, flatbed letterpress printing, low-relief rubber-blanket offset press printing, and high-speed, web-fed newspaper printing.

ETCHING: Its Origins and Process

Etching is a printmaking process in which the artist/printmaker draws an image onto a metal plate that has previously been coated with a thin layer of waxy acid-resistant material (*ground)*. The act of drawing (usually with an etcher's needle) cuts lines through the wax barrier and exposes the metal. When the plate is immersed in an acid bath, the drawn image will be dissolved into the metal surface by the etching action of the acid. Areas still protected by the ground will remain unaffected.

When the ground is removed with solvent, the etched plate will have grooves where the lines were initially drawn through the waxy coating. The printmaker covers the surface of the plate with a stiff paste ink, wipes it clean in stages using the clean-cut edge of a piece of cardboard as a squeegee, then cheese cloth (tarlatan), the palm of the hand, and sometimes paper, so that ink remains only in the etched grooves. The plate is then laid on the bed of a roller-etching press and covered with dampened printmaking paper.

Three different blankets are laid on top of the paper; a thin felt sizing catcher to absorb water from the paper, a woven pusher blanket for stability, and a thick felt cushion blanket to keep the pressure even. This stack is then run between the rollers of an etching press with enough pressure to push the paper into the etched grooves and pick out the ink. When the bed of the press has passed through the rollers and the blankets have been removed, the finished impression can be peeled up from the plate, examined, and dried.

Since this process prints from grooves or textures beneath the virgin surface, impressions from this process are called intaglio prints. There are essentially two categories of intaglio prints. If the image is created in the plate using hand tools, it is generally considered an engraving. If acid is used to create the image in the plate, then the print is generally considered an etching.

Medieval European armorers and goldsmiths developed engraving or the craft of insizing metal with various hand tools. The use of acid to do the difficult handwork of insizing was an invention that sprang from their craft during the mid 1400's as paper became more available throughout Europe.

It is easy to see how the development of the craft of printing intaglio images could come from a metalsmith's desire to proof the progress of his work, keep a record of his design for himself, and have something to show his patron before the final metal work was done. It is not known who actually invented the technique. Some guild craftsman probably struck on the brilliant idea of rubbing a mixture of thick oil and charcoal into his metal work, wiping off the excess, laying a piece of paper on the metal, and burnishing the back of the paper to transfer the oil image.

As proofing the craftsman's work became more common, it would be only a minor step to begin appreciating the paper proof as a sufficient end product, giving rise to etching as a new art medium.

The imagery in this book is my particular permutation of both the relief and etching print processes, and the invention of paper.

THE ARTIST'S RELIEF PRINT PERMUTATIONS
Their History and Description

I gravitated toward the printmaking media in my college studies during the academic years 1968-69. I was captivated by the notion of a democratic art form that could, like a pie, be made with consistent quality and yet be physically shared with many individuals. Maybe the pie notion appealed to me because I knew how much time and passion I was willing to invest in an image if I felt its gestalt warranted the effort. Also,

I wasn't sufficiently convinced that I could get even minimum wages out of my labor if I had to recoup all my investment from the sale of a single work. This conflict was no doubt caused by an early apprehension on my part about the fickle and prodigal nature of art market politics.

I had been a self-directed art student even before the facilities for learning such skills became available to me. When they finally did, I dove into the various print media for three years, assessing what I liked and disliked about each medium. In that time I more or less settled on etching and lithography as prime media, although neither of these processes scratched the exact spot in my visual aesthetics where I itched the most.

I loved the delicious tonal/textural drawing surface of a properly surfaced German limestone; however, the larger one wishes to make an image, the more prohibitive the weight of the drawing surface becomes. Also, it is risky to do fine work on a stone without knowing how it will react chemically. This means that you either have to own the stone you are working on long enough to learn its chemical idiosyncrasies, or be limited by a school or commercial atelier facility where the stones you want to work on are located.

I finally ended up owning five different litho-stones. It must be some kind of testament to my dedication that I nearly gave myself a hernia carrying them back and forth between my home studio, where I did the drawing, and the school's printing facility.

Etching and the intaglio media had exciting visual features. I especially liked the rich, velvet tones of aquatint and the gamesmanship of linear drawing notation, which to me had the risk and bravado of high-stakes watercolor painting. I was also drawn to the pronounced embossing left by the plate in sumptuous cotton-rag paper. But again, there was a distinct size limitation.

This time it wasn't a weight problem but a problem of skin. One of the steps in inking an etching plate requires the printmaker to hand wipe the image just before printing--sort of a final tune-up. In my senior year, I worked on an edition from a 24″ x 36″ inch plate only to find my hands had lost their palm skin down to the ouch layer. Although the range of achievable effects in the relief woodblock and linoleum print processes were somewhat limiting, I knew that roller inking in the relief media had a solid advantage over losing so much hand skin.

By the summer of 1970, I was wondering if there wasn't some way to combine what I liked about all of the processes into one new print-making method. I started experimenting with industrial materials and asking questions of people in the commercial printing trades.

I tried various ways of printing metal and paper offset plates. I experimented with direct drawing on silk screen, making and printing polymer photoplastic relief plates, and finally relief photo etching.

By that time, I had drawn on a wide range of surfaces and concluded that no traditional print-making surface could effectively provide the kind of textural imagery I was looking for. I had seen drawings of sports figures in the newspaper that had been done on a likely surface, so I explored this new potential. The texture in the newspaper drawings came from a thick, embossed paper called *coquille board*.

In the winter of 1971, I experimented on a sheet of it. After trying various drawing tools, I settled on wax pencils because they yielded a clean, high contrast drawing. Also, because they were wax, there was less chance of the drawing becoming smeared. For my purposes, Berol or Eagle Prismacolor pencils turned out to be the kings of coquille drawing. They gave me the rich drawing texture I had been searching for, and I knew that I had one piece of my new printmaking process in hand.

I found that I had to spray coat each drawing

done with these wax pencils, as soon as possible after completion, with a good quality plastic spray like Grumbacher Tuffilm because the wax had a tendency to oxidize and lose some of the contrast it needed to make a good negative.

My next objective was to transfer a finished image to a printable surface. Early in the spring of 1972, I completed a 22″ x 30″ coquille drawing of a *'48 Plymouth* (page 115) that I had seen on one of my desert rambles. I took my completed drawing to a friend who operated a copy camera and worked at a printing company. We made several exposures and proofed them until he was sure he couldn't get any closer to the center of my tonal range.

I took the best looking negative of the group, laid it on a light table, continued removing unwanted dots with opaquing paint and adding detail by scratching off emulsion with an x-acto knife in areas where I felt I could improve on the camera's limitations. I corrected and proofed my negative until I was satisfied it would give me the image I wanted on a plate. It occurred to me later that these efforts to alter and perfect the negative were an exact parallel to the traditional process of correcting and proofing an etching plate, with the exception that this new method was allowing corrections that were both very precise and much easier.

I had had a chance to experiment with photo-lacquer-coated magnesium plates the previous summer during a stay in Boulder, Colorado, which led me to favor it as printer matrix. I took my freshly preened negative to the plate technician and asked him what he thought.

He said that together we could probably get something usable from it. He laid my negative, emulsion side down, over an unexposed photo-etching plate in a glass-fronted vacuum exposure case, closed the lid, and turned on the vacuum.

The vacuum pump sucked the air out of the space between the glass, the negative, and the plate, causing the necessary tight contact that would yield a sharp image. He exposed the light-sensitive lacquer coating on the plate through the negative with an intense arc lamp for about three minutes. He then immersed the exposed plate in a tank of developer solution. The developer chemically softened the photo lacquer that had not received light because it was shielded by the remaining opaque areas of the negative. He told me that wherever light passed through the clear parts of the negative, it set the lacquer so that the developer would not soften it.

He pulled the developed plate out of the tank in about four minutes, set it on a special wooden rack in a large sink, and sprayed it down with water. The blue lacquer seemed to bleed away, revealing my drawn image in acid resist on a background of silvery magnesium. The plate was ready to be etched.

An etching machine looks like a large square stainless steel suitcase on a heavy metal stand. On the inside of the lid is a slow-turning, motor-powered clamp. The lower part looks like a tank with foos-ball paddles immersed in acid. The technician clamped my plate face down to the rotor, closed the lid, and turned on the machine.

As the plate slowly turned horizontally in the machine, the paddles would flip a nitric acid compound solution up against the plate, causing a very controlled dissolving of the metal from the now upside-down image surface.

It took about twenty minutes to etch the image to a depth of a 32nd of an inch in the 16-gauge metal. After the plate was removed, neutralized and trimmed, I filed a traditional etching plate bevel around the perimeter so that the plate would not cut the paper when it went through the press. I knew that I would have to do a little additional hand engraving on the etched plate to get it to print exactly what I wanted, but that was to be expected.

Later that afternoon I surface rolled the plate

with litho-ink and a rubber roller that looks like a large rolling pin. I set the plate on the bed of an etching press, laid the dampened paper and blankets down just as I would have for a normal intaglio etching, ran the stack through the press, and created my first relief etching.

When I pulled off the blankets, I noticed that the paper had become molded to the plate. I wondered how that first Chinese relief print, nineteen hundred years before, appeared to the eyes of its inventor. When I peeled the paper away from the plate and held the new print up in oblique light, I was pleasantly surprised to see how well the embossing that I had seen from the other side worked within the image area.

I had never before witnessed such an intricately embossed effect within a printed image. It was as though I had just been ushered into a unique marriage of paper and ink.

Needless to say, I was delighted. I felt as if I finally had a process that could give me both visual power and delicacy. My new relief etching process turned out to be a quantum leap for the kind of images I wanted to do.

Since that spring afternoon in 1972, I have hand-printed the thirty editioned images in this book. All of them in varying degrees have this same embossed effect. It is the signature fingerprint of this new relief etching process and my particular contribution to the world of fine printmaking.

COQUILLE DU NOIR AND COQUILLE DU BLANC
Permutations from the New Print Process

The coquille paperboard that I used to create twenty-six of the images in this collection was difficult to correct without destroying the very texture that made the unique drawings possible. While a light cleaning with a soft white eraser wouldn't affect the embossed surface, trying to remove parts of a wax Prismacolor rendering could erode the coquille texture and threaten the consistent re-draw ability in the corrected area.

No matter how well one plans a labor-intensive image in advance, corrections are inevitable. The very fact that an artist grows visually between the beginning and end of a lengthy work ensures this. The drawings were taking between 80 and 250 hours to finish and could be destroyed by one inopportune mistake. I eased through these difficult passages as carefully as I could. After completing 14 drawings, however, I was feeling like a freestyle rock climber who was seriously pushing his luck.

I began working and testing tougher surfaces on which to draw. After a few months of looking, painting, spraying, drawing, and scratching on a range of papers and boards, I toughened the existing coquille surface in two ways. I decided to proceed with an idea that had been hanging around on the backporch of my thoughts for a couple of years. I wanted to draw in pure white on a rich black surface. In my experiments, I came across a naphtha-based, carbon-black stencil ink, manufactured by Marsh-Tennessee. I layer sprayed this ink on the coquille board, and it strengthened the surface and added a nice tooth to the embossed texture.

When I drew on this new surface with a 938 white Prismacolor or a 164T Berol white china marker, the effect was a pure white on a rich dense black. Not only did the drawing effect look very promising, but this combination was just what the film in the copy camera was designed for. Negatives from these drawings required fewer corrections, and my new medium had the additional advantage of being more tractable.

I could not erase the white wax once it had been drawn or it would have smudged into the texture of the carbon ink coating. The only way to make corrections was to place cellophane tape over the image, then redraw what needed to be deleted with a small ball-end stylus. The tape would stick to the unwanted wax, and if I carefully lifted the tape, the wax would come up without seriously affecting the carbon ink surface.

There were a limited number of times I could do this without pulling the carbon ink off, but the new process gave me a comfortable margin of error. In extreme cases small portions of the board could be re-sprayed with the stencil ink.

The Berol china-marker could be corrected, but since the wax was much softer, corrections were difficult. I used these pencils only in the finishing stages of the drawing to maximize highlights. I named this new drawing medium COQUILLE DU NOIR (coquille from black). *Back To Nature* (page 43) was the first image I completed using this process. It was finished in the early fall of 1985, and the first prints were done in March of 1986.

If I wanted to draw a black image on a white background, I would spray the coquille board with a medium coat of high quality, gloss-white enamel, being very careful to coat the surface but not fill in the coquille texture. I would allow the enamel to harden for two days before beginning to draw. Because there was so little tooth to the enamel, a deep black was difficult to achieve. However, this surface proved to be very tough and worked well with the 935 Prismacolor black. The cellophane tape could correct any errors with remarkable precision and cleanliness.

I named this second medium COQUILLE DU BLANC (coquille from white). Negatives from Coquille du Blanc drawings were as problem-free as those drawn on COQUILLE DU NOIR. The first drawing I did in this new medium was *First Lessons In Conversational Truck* (page 99). It was finished in the late winter of 1985, and the first prints were pulled in July of 1986.

ETCHING IN THE DIGITAL AGE
Giving Ancient Crafts a High Tech Edge

As I continued to grow technically, my coquille drawings became ever more subtle and detailed. In the autumn of 1988, I ran into an unforeseen wall with the *The Ides of Gratification* (page 107). The fine textures in this COQUILLE DU NOIR process rendering had become too detailed for standard copy camera technology. Even when I enlarged the image on the negative to the maximum size that would fit on a 22″ x 30″ Arches Cover sheet, neither the negative nor plate emulsions could capture the texture. I had completed an otherwise good drawing that my existing technology was unable to transfer to a plate.

This realization was very troubling because, at the time, I was under a production schedule to finish as many drawings as possible during that calendar year. The solution to my dilemma came when I decided to have a continuous-tone negative made from my drawing. The negative image was then digitized on a drum scanner.

Putting my image into the digital realm and manipulating the contrast in a computer was the only way to preserve the extended range of highlight and shadow detail that the COQUILLE DU NOIR medium was capable of producing. *The Ides Of Gratification* may be the world's first hand-printed digitally mastered etching.

The best things in civilization are arrived at by the same methodical layers of adaptation and discovery. To me there are few things in life as fascinating as quests like these. Once you are involved in a successful discovery, it is hard to think as small as you did before it happened.

The Mindscape

A Marriage of Sensory Perception and Imagination

It can be both revealing and unsettling to reconstruct the events and choices that have brought any of us to our current state in life. The story of how I, as a visual artist, came to be involved with words and writing begins with my father and his unusual collection of typewritten thoughts, poems, and essays, kept in an old, cloth-bound metal post ledger.

He would come home after midnight, having worked the swing shift, and sit in his carpet-upholstered chair, typing by kitchen light into the wee hours of the morning. Some idea would have come to him as he stood working at the printing press that could not wait for sleep.

He never told me where he got the impetus to keep such a journal. Although his schooling ended at the tenth grade, he read a great deal. Perhaps that was the source of his inspirations. Maybe he had a subconscious wish to be a writer but knew that he could never support a family on hopes like that. He wrote few poems, which I found memorable, and even a captivating short story or two. His experience of the Depression probably chilled any entrepreneurial inclinations he had, and, to my knowledge, his writing was just a private thing he did.

Although my mother was always writing to her friends in a neat cursive hand, I rarely got the chance to read or hear what she had written. So, it was most likely my father, who thought nothing of waking me up at three in the morning on school days to read me his latest effort fresh from the kitchen chair think tank, who modeled the passions of writing for me.

The same gene that has inclined my choices toward creativity for forty years or more, like a life-affirming addiction, could just as well have been showing up in his mid-life experience as a propensity to write.

Although I was encouraged into the world of visual art, it seems as though a love of language tagged along, even though I didn't sense it until I was in my early twenties. My love for words rose to the surface of my creative activity in the spring of 1967.

I had started a series of graphite drawings, inspired by my intrigue with the history of the abandoned mining towns and railroad lines of California, Nevada, Arizona, Utah, and Colorado. Whenever I had time off and enough money, I went exploring this great desert region to see how those who had lived there survived in the inconvenient places. There was a compelling mystery in the potential images I was seeing out there that seemed to get right down to a glamour-free, bottom-line reality. It seemed to me that the marrow of life could be viewed more honestly through the survivors and ruined remains of such places.

The drawing series finally grew to eleven images and took two-and-a-half years to finish. The time it took to do each piece gave me ample opportunity to ruminate about the places I was rendering so carefully. As I was drawing my images, the ruminations seemed to come to me with the compression of poetry or short story narratives.

These words not only seemed to actualize the visual experience of my image, but they could also transcend the border of the drawing in both time and space, revealing a kind of imaginative extrapolation. Because the experience began in the visual realm, these extrapolations seemed somehow more cognitively interactive--more intimate than the relationship between book or magazine stories and traditional illustration.

The extrapolation process was very often as interesting as the visual work itself. I began to write down these ruminations so that I might be able to share similar experiences with others. For lack of a better moniker, I called these *concurrent texts* "Poetics," more because they seemed to work for the same kind of drama, compression, and emotional focus as poetry than any attempt on my part to conform to a specific literary paradigm.

There seemed to be an intriguing parallel between the actual two-dimensional flatness of my images, which had the artistic illusion of a third dimension, and substantive poetry, which reaches us as compressed language and then expands to a three-dimensional experience as it comes into contact with our imagination. I looked for other parallels between aesthetic media and began to have a keen interest in how such latent synergies might be developed and utilized as another form of art expression.

During or immediately after I had finished one of these early drawings, I would write out a first draft of words. Then I would work on the effect between my new image and its text. I did this for ten of the eleven drawings in the series and made a small edition of reproductions, each image with its respective text on a separate sheet. Then I went looking for an audience. A signature example from this early series (facing page) is entitled "The Weed."

The Weed

Between a narrow hill
and dreams of El Dorado,
someone had put in hard time
making a rough spanning gesture.
Scrap wood and shoring
manhandled,
hammered in,
ties and rail laid down--
they needed something
to keep the growing burden
of worthless rock
from choking
their only road out.

Then continuing,
with sledges and star drills,
they bored into the colorful
ribbon vein.
After the blasting and dust,
they mucked out.
Some loads, smiling like payday
toward the transport chutes,
but more loads,
like tired workday men,
groaned across
the tenuous span.

As they tipped each hopper up,
mud and cobbles
spilled down the hill--
a sliding angry rush
of clattering debris
was added to that cairn of losses
growing just beyond
their porthole to imagined glory.

Back in the cool dark,
the walls wept an ooze
of rich mineral blood.
The floor of the hole
ran red with muddy water
that thinned as it left the tunnel
into a sinuous stream
only to vanish once again
into the steep fallow earth.

For a thousand feet or more in,
they labored hard
at the receding rock face.
Drilling, grunting, cussing--
most of the countless tons of hole
ended up as steel scree flanks
on the hill beyond the trestle.

Then one day,
they came out of the tunnel
and with drawn faces
left it forever.

For many turns of autumn,
windstorms lifted up
great clouds of dust
from the valley floor.
The tunnel walls ceased to weep
but left red iron traces
draped long down the hillside
like an ancient wound.

The dust
from its nomad ventures
settled in--
sifting down
among the ragged cobbles
and
sometime after
the early cycles
of gentle spring rain,
a weed grew.

Chloride, Arizona, 1968

The Weed

My part-time entrepreneurial venture kept me in spending money during my first three years of college. I took a hiatus from writing *texts* during my senior year of undergraduate study because I was learning a whole range of new printmaking processes.

The hiatus continued into graduate school for much the same reason, though by then I was already developing my own relief etching process. I recall thinking that the new relief imagery would be a "natural" for my *poetic/concurrent text* idea.

One of the third-quarter prerequisites at the university I was attending required graduate candidates to present an art folio of their recent work to a review board so they might determine whether the work was of sufficient quality for the student to continue graduate studies.

As I submitted my first semester and undergraduate work complete with many drawings, some with their *texts*, I was a bit apprehensive but eager to demonstrate what I had discovered about images, words, and imagination. They conferred for about fifteen minutes and then told me that I was in a solid position to continue my graduate work.

Delighted by this affirmation, I offered to recite the words to one of my images for them. When I had finished reciting, they told me that, while they didn't claim to know a great deal about poetry, they did know that putting visual images and words together was decidedly "de'-classe'."

They told me that visual art should stand alone as a discrete experience without such embellishments. Although I was disappointed at this response, their rationale had a sort of "father knows best" authority. I took their expert word on the subject and ceased to write for my images.

For fourteen years following that event, my writing energies as a graduate student and an art instructor went into reports, proposals, course descriptions, position statements, and essays. For my own love of words, I would occasionally write a song and play it on my guitar for friends or to the twilight walls of my living room.

During that time I completed twenty major coquille drawings and had finished printing the full sheet relief etching editions for fourteen of them. I was, however, left with an empty longing to explore with words the imaginary time and space I had experienced before I had become "academically sophisticated." That longing tended to manifest itself as a desire to explain what moved me to do a particular image whenever there was someone who cared enough to ask. What triggered my second writing renaissance was just such an interest.

One winter afternoon in the fall of 1986, I gathered up a month's worth of bachelor laundry and headed off to the laundromat. On the way I stopped to see Kim Peden at his dental lab and deliver my most recent etching for his collection. He took a break from the grinding and polishing wheels, and we started a friendly conversation that eventually got around to why I did what I did.

He pointed to *Sierra Before the Storm* and said, "Take that one, for instance. What's the philosophy behind that image?" My explanation began like a leak forming in an earthen dam that had backed up a mountain river for far too long.

"Geeze, man," Kim noted when I was through, "that's good. You should write that down; maybe have it printed for your collectors so they can frame it up next to the etching." I thanked him for his advice, told him I'd give it my best shot, and we'd see what came out.

The washers were barely staying in balance as I sat in a plastic chair scratching my head. On a legal pad, I had been trying to plow through what had all the earmarks of becoming a very boring essay about the soul of visual art and the purpose of human creative motivations.

All of a sudden I woke up. I realized that the *poetic/concurrent texts* I had done years before offered a perfect resolution. I didn't need to cover my behind with the same kind of seamless political dogma I had been turning out for my job. Besides, who in their right mind would choose to read through a new sports car owner's manual instead of getting into the bucket seat and taking the car for a spin in the country?

The solution was so obvious that I felt like yelling, "Eureka!" But, unlike Archimedes, I had not waited so long to do my laundry. I wadded up my philosophical hen scratchings along with the myopic paradigm of my graduate professors and threw them into the trash can.

I took a deep breath, stood up and transferred my damp clothes to the dryers, fed in quarters, and started them spinning. I sat back down with a clean sheet of paper. What was long overdue and seriously needed here was solid "poetic" soul. So, with the dryers flopping the damp clothing around, buttons clicking and scraping against the windows, I began my first *poetic text* in fourteen years, shocked that so much water had passed under the bridge. At the top of the page I wrote, *Sierra Before the Storm*.

With the writing of this *text* (see page 16), I began to reconsider a rationale for artistic activity that focuses on and explores the potential synergy in the spaces between cultural media disciplines. I eventually began to call the finished products of my exploration *mindscapes*.

Although I rejected my graduate professors' admonitions, I knew there were good reasons for their apprehensions about combining visual and literary forms. Just so that I would not overlook or forget their valid and unspoken reservations, I established a production standard for all of these symbiotic creations. The rule states that the various component expressions of a *mindscape* should be able to stand alone, without the support of the other components. In other words, the visual, the *concurrent text*, the music, and any other work included should all be cut from the same quality of fabric.

The process of assembling various kinds of *mindscapes* into book form has created new potentials. The first inkling that a coffee table book of collected relief etchings and their *concurrent texts* might be the most suitable vehicle for this new kind of experience occurred to me in the spring of 1986. I recalled reciting my fledgling "poetics" to whole rooms of people in community art shows back in the late 60's and seeing their positive reactions to that experience.

I decided that it was time to work some of my newer *texts* into a form of oral drama. Pursuing that inclination, I went into Stephen Bigger's sound studio in the fall of 1986. We laid down a series of recitations and song tracks. After I left, he added reverb, equalization, and musical accompaniment. About three months later, he handed me a tape of our collaboration. For a first try, the effect was marvelous. I was hooked on the idea of taking my words into the audio realm. In the spring of 1991 I was finally able to get back into a sound studio, where I could further explore images and words in a sound medium.

The rapid growth of digital audio technology from the mid 80's to late 90's has facilitated many of my ideas and explorations. I can create audio-worlds in my small studio at home that would have required a very large sound stage when I first began writing.

During the summer of 1991, I made my first sound camera with a tripod, a stereo microphone, and a DAT (digital audio tape) machine. I took this makeshift rig and went on an extensive road trip throughout the Southwest. The idea was to gather CD quality sounds in those places where I was inspired to draw each of the images in this book. I likened myself to a Navajo sand painter gathering colors to use in a painting ceremony.

By bringing these sounds back into a digital studio, I could load them into the computer's memory, then mix and use them like paint on a pallet to create audio landscapes. Against these audio stage sets, I could perform the oral drama for each *text*.

I began composing the music for this project in 1994, and by 1996, I had completed more than enough music to use as introductions and segues for the audio landscapes.

Not only has this project given me the chance to create works that are customarily segregated art forms, but also it has necessitated that I fuse them into one tangible platform. In that process of fusion, every *Roadsongs* monograph becomes a conceptual art vehicle--another work of art. For this reason, every example in the first edition is hand-signed and serially numbered, like the relief etchings that sparked this long creative progression.

The book was designed so that you could go into the quiet of your own listening environment, sit back in comfort, put the CDs on the player, look at an image and let the audio landscapes, the music, the narration, and the drama, transport you beyond the borders of my imagery into places that exist only within your mind. With this book and your imagination, the moving synergy of the *mindscape* can open the door to an experience that at once is both shared and uniquely private.

I hope that your experience of this art may at some point parallel my own. This true sharing of experience may only happen occasionally. I have had complete strangers who, after viewing one of my images, came up and told me the very thoughts I was thinking while in the heat of creating it. I have seen deep emotion in the faces of my viewers in public places where such overt displays would normally be embarrassing. I am moved by these incidents because this is exactly the kind of meaningful connection I look for in my personal aesthetic encounters, whether they are inspired by man or nature.

I do not subscribe to the notion that there is only one way of seeing a work of art, nor do I want my viewers to feel that the genetic idea behind these images is, in any way, intended to limit their own perceptions. To be critically thinking humans, we need to seek our own meanings in all we view.

For me, it is the tractive ability of an image to draw the viewer in and communicate on many levels that determines whether a work of art finally matters. The determination of how well I have done my work will reside personally with those individuals who participate in the extended experience that this art was made to generate. For those who engage in the *mindscape* experience, I want to assure you that the road map to get you into that personal imaginative dialogue was the very best that I could have drawn.

Malcolm Graeme Childers
The Artist and His Work

Eric Hobson

Malcolm was born on the 19th of February 1945, in Riverside, California. As a child he was blessed with an exploratory nature. This natural curiosity, and the experiences that it provided, showed up later as an inclination to make art. This artistic inclination was strongly encouraged by his father, and the place where he lived was rich in visually stimulating subjects.

Riverside in the late 40's, 50's and 60's was a landscape of inspiring contrasts. Within easy viewing were wide vistas ringed with majestic mountains, rolling foothills, fields, and citrus orchards. His early drawings show the strong influence of that landscape. His interest in art continued through childhood with encouragement from many sources, and by the time he reached his early twenties, he had developed an impressive drawing and painting skill.

In 1968, Malcolm returned from Viet Nam and began formal art training at Riverside Community College. He completed the work for his Bachelor of Arts degree at Humboldt State University in Northern California. During his last two undergraduate years, he began to focus his studies on drawing, printmaking, and photography.

He continued that focus when he returned to Southern California and completed his Master of Arts degree at Fullerton State University in 1973. He was one of only two graduating art students who had a job waiting for him at graduation. In 1974, he took a position as drawing, painting, printmaking, and photography instructor at Southern College, near Chattanooga, Tennessee. In addition to his regular schedule, he taught adjunct classes at Cleveland State College and the University of Tennessee at Chattanooga.

He taught for thirteen years at the college level and became an Associate Professor. During that time, he created eleven of the images in this book and traveled extensively throughout the U.S. and Canada, getting a feel for the landscape, its nature, and our current human condition.

By 1986 he had come to the conviction that a personal art statement dealing with human values and their effect on this Earth was necessary to inform, organize, and justify his continuing involvement in the arts. As a result of his angst, in the months between August 1986 and May 1987, he conceived and outlined a massive work of conceptual art which he subsequently titled,

A GATHERING OF HORIZONS.

Developed in the mid 60's, conceptual art is an art form that shifts the intentional content or meaning of the created work away from tangible objects, like a drawing, painting or sculpture, to a concept or idea that motivates the expression. Conceptual art is the art form of ideas.

In this arena, the artist might make art objects, but they exist solely to support the art idea as the focus of the work. When experiencing a work of conceptual art, the viewer will most likely be reading a description and looking at documentary photographs or other evidences of the idea.

Malcolm chose this form because it was the only arena that could handle the gravity and scale of the art idea that he wished to express. That idea can be easily understood by following his philosophic thought progression:

A. Meaning and human values do not exist without consciousness.

B. Art is a human word. All art, whether by creation or designation, has that status conferred on it by human consciousness.

C. Since there is significant scientific evidence that humanity originated from the Earth, it is safe to conclude that all of our aesthetic expressions, visual or otherwise, have also originated from our Earth-based experience. The Earth is, therefore, the source of all art.

D. In the past we humans have believed that the Earth's resources were inexhaustible, and we consumed them accordingly. Now it is obvious that we are wastefully using up our biosphere of origins faster than it can recover. It is time to reorient both our lives, our values, and our aesthetic expressions to honor and preserve that which sustains all of us.

E. We humans have already established ethical standards for preserving those things that we value most. Irreplaceable art masterpieces should be protected from destructive environmental influences. They should be maintained and enjoyed in a safe, peaceful place, and restored in the event of damage.

F. Should we not have at least the same regard for our planet of origins? Should we not reverentially endow it with the same long-term conservation status that we give to our most irreplaceable art treasures?

In consummation of these ideas, on the 20th of April 1987, Malcolm Childers formally declared and signed this conceptual art expression:

"THE PLANET EARTH IS A WORK OF ART"

In order to give his conceptual expression both credible material and aesthetic evidence, he created the U.S. 111th Meridian Project. Malcolm chose the corridor of land between the 110th and 112th Meridians as an *E Pluribus Unum* sample of the Planet Earth. He decided to place monuments at both borders and photograph the terrain, environment and culture within the corridor to demonstrate adequately the gravity of his conceptual art expression.

The project, as he envisioned it, would require investment, business counsel, and promotion. Malcolm approached William Ackerman (then CEO of Windham Hill Records) through Philip Aaberg, a Windham Hill composer/musician. Windham Hill lent credentials to the project.

Malcolm and I first met in my office one afternoon in the spring of 1987. He was seeking advice about managing and marketing his idea. It took him about four months to assemble the needed funding for the 111th Meridian Project. As soon as he had it, he packed his gear and drove from Tennessee to Montana.

On the 2nd of June 1987, at about 2:00 in the afternoon, he planted a time capsule on the Canadian border junction with the 111th Meridian, in Liberty County, Montana.

During that month, he made his way south, crossing back and forth, along his Meridian corridor through Montana, Idaho, Wyoming, Utah, and Arizona toward the Mexican border, taking both aerial and ground photographs.

On the 25th of June, Malcolm buried a second capsule on the U.S.-Mexican border, describing the philosophy of his planet sampling effort. During that inaugural journey, he took over

3,000 photographs, the highlights of which he hopes to publish in an annotated collection.

Although his conceptual work was sufficiently documented when the second time capsule was set on the 25th of June, he has continued to photograph his Meridian sample. For Malcolm this corridor epitomizes "the art" that the Earth is.

What Malcolm found most memorable in this 100 mile-wide by 1250 mile-long corridor is also apparent in his photographs. The images show:

~ The great diversity of landforms, cultures, and ecosystems that exist along his 111th Meridian sample.

~ How insignificant we as individuals actually appear against the backdrop of that expansive and majestic landscape.

~ How remarkably effective we humans are at making vast changes for benefit or harm within that thin envelope of the Earth's biosphere where, up to now, all known life exists.

Before Malcolm began this conceptual work, he was confronted by the futility of making more visual art while what he considered to be the inspirational source of all art was at significant risk of degradation and destruction. By declaring the planet Earth a work of art, he revalues and reorients the arts in their service to humanity.

Faced with our continuing threat to and extinction of other species, Malcolm has chosen to refocus his ideas about what ought to be considered priceless or irreplaceable art treasures.

In the wake of his 111th Meridian experience, he says that he can't even talk about current "art issues" without feeling "like a guy with a brewski in his hand, arguing football scores while his house burns down around him."

The task of getting us to place our highest aesthetic values on the real natural beauty of the living Earth is well beyond the scope of any one man. Thankfully, there are many other voices who realize the gravity of this aesthetic imperative. Malcolm figures this work of art will be finished when every human treats the living Earth as though it were a masterpiece--with the regard that will allow it to sustain its rich diversity of life indefinitely.

Six months after he returned from his *111th Meridian* journey, Malcolm and I formed the Wind River Corporation, an art production and holding company. I became involved in his work as a management adviser during the completion of his six most recent relief etching images and a principal in this book's production. In 1998, I commissioned Malcolm to create *Windows on American Light*, a seventy-two piece museum-grade photographic collection.

In his career, Malcolm has been invited to show his work in over 100 regional and national juried exhibitions where he has won numerous awards. His works have been collected by many museums, private and corporate collections.

In February 1993, Malcolm married Pamela Barnard Farrell, a nationally-recognized writing instructor, consultant and poet. The author of numerous articles, chapters, and professional books, Pamela has her doctorate in education. Pamela and Malcolm are currently working on books, art projects, and workshops that focus on visual literacy, writing, and the development of critical and creative thinking.

Mark Caldwell for Wind River Productions

Notes on the Music from ROADSONGS

All of the words and music on the two *Roadsongs* CD's were written by Malcolm Graeme Childers except *"ROCK AMERICA,"* which is Miles Aubrey's feedback electric guitar variation on the anthem by Katherine Lee Bates. All of the narration and voice acting was performed by the author except for the voice of the waitress performed by May Wood in THE SEMI, and the ambiences acted by the Thomas Francescon family in NEVADA NORTHERN FREIGHT #81, HIGH BAROQUE FOR THE HEARTLAND, and SUNDOWN ON THE DARKSIDE OF THE MOON. All of the music was arranged by Stephen Bigger or Dan Landrum except *"OUT ON THE HIGHWAY,"* arranged by Stephen Ray Wells, and *"IN THE DUST OF DREAMS,"* arranged by the author.

The following is a music and audio performance list.

BEGINNING OF AUDIO CD ONE

Soliloquy AT A CROSSROADS ON STATE 38 (pages 12-14)

1. *"ANOTHER MAN'S SUNRISE"* (Malcolm Childers/Dan Landrum, MIDI keyboards and samplers)--
An introductory road-fugue for two guitars and strings sounds........1:15
Monologue SIERRA BEFORE THE STORM (page 18)

2. *"YOU AN' ME BABY"* (Stephen Bigger, piano, bass and drums; Miles Aubrey, electric guitar; Don Thompson, vocals)--An emblematic rock song segues into the solo/choral invocation (Malcolm Childers, keyboards)...........:42

3. *"DID WE GET ALL THAT WE WANTED? / LIVE ON"* (Stephen Bigger, director; Chris Aymes, soloist; Rise' Gustafson, Kimolin Crutcher, Stephen and Susan Bigger, LaFredrick Thirkill, singers).........2:23
Monologue NEVADA NORTHERN FREIGHT #81 (pages 20-22)

4a. *"OUT ON THE HIGHWAY"* (Steve Wells, bass, drums, keyboard, rhythm and lead guitars; Jeff Larsen, pedal steel; Ward Stout, fiddle; Chris Aymes, soloist; Ellen Wells, harmonies)--
A 'how truckin' saved me after you' country song (first verse)........1:35
Audio drama ONYX STORE (pages 24-26)

4b. *"OUT ON THE HIGHWAY"*--(final verse)........1:15
Audio drama THE SEMI, PETERBILT (pages 28-32). *"OUT ON THE HIGHWAY"* finale' provides an interlude as the drivers enter the infamous coffee shop de l'amore.
Audio drama FRENCHY'S FLATHEAD FLYER ON THE RIGHT DAY (pages 34-36)
Audio drama ON THE CUTTING EDGE OF TEMPORARY (pages (38-40)

5. *"A SOUTHWIND DESCRIBES THE PLAINS"* (Malcolm Childers/Dan Landrum, MIDI keyboards and samplers)--A melodic description for orchestral string sounds and the wind........2:16
Audio drama BACK TO NATURE (pages 42-44)
Audio drama "ASCENT FROM #3" (pages 46-48)

6. *"THROUGH A WINDOW OF DAWN"* (Malcolm Childers/Dan Landrum, bowed psaltry, MIDI string samples)--An etude for the price of freedom........1:14
Monologue AMID THE BEAMS AND RUST OF DAYS GONE BY (page 50)

7a. *"COMING DOWN FROM EL DORADO"* (Dan Landrum, hammer dulcimer)--An anthem for miners............:50
Monologue "WOODEN MASTODON" (pages 56-56)

7b. *"COMING DOWN FROM EL DORADO"* (Kirk Johnson, harmonica)--Reprise........1:18
Audio drama "DARWIN ARCO SERVICE" (pages 58-60)

END OF AUDIO CD ONE........Total time CD ONE........71:27

BEGINNING OF AUDIO CD TWO

1. *"A WALK IN THE HEARTLAND TWILIGHT"* (Malcolm Childers/Dan Landrum, MIDI keyboards and samplers)--A guitar and string air for small-town America........1:00
   Audio drama HIGH BAROQUE FOR THE HEARTLAND (pages 62-64) ending with the song,
2. *"DEAR LORD YOU KNOW"* (Stephen Bigger, piano and organ; Kimolin Crutcher, vocals)--A benediction for the soul of religious broadcasting........1:40
   Monologue A FUNERAL FOR VENUS (page 66)
3. *"FOR HOPE OF LOVE"*(Stephen Bigger, piano)--A reverie for piano and passing storm........1:16
   Monologue over audio drama DESDICHADO: AN ECHO OF STOLEN THUNDER (page 70)
4. *"IN THE DUST OF DREAMS"* (Malcolm Childers, MIDI sampler)--An etude for what remains........1:04
   Audio drama TALKIN' DURANGO FLUES (pages 74-76)
5. *"BACKROAD BAGATELLE"* (Kirk Johnson, harmonica)--An air for the vagabond spirit........1:17
   Monologue THE FLATCAR, BLANCA, COLORADO (pages 78-80)
6. *"A VIEW ON WHITE MOUNTAINS"* (Stephen Bigger, piano)--A muse for great heights........1:00
   Monologue THE ROCK ISLAND LINE, NEAR ITS VANISHING POINT (pages 82-84)
   Monologue S.P. DIESEL #3665 (pages 86-88)
7. *"JUST IN PASSING"* (Malcolm Childers/Dan Landrum, MIDI keyboards and samplers)--An interlude for guitar and string sounds and a moving freight train........1:00
   Audio drama '53 BUICK ROADMASTER (pages 90-92)
8. *"REFLECTIONS AT DAY'S END"* (Stephen Bigger, piano)--A transparent air for the fine art of memory........1:00
   Monologue ORO GRANDE MARKET (pages 94-96)
9. *"ROCK AMERICA" (*Miles Aubrey, electric guitar; Stephen Bigger, keyboard)--A feedback guitar blends with strings sounds on the great anthem. 1:00
   Audio drama FIRST LESSONS IN CONVERSATIONAL TRUCK (pages 98-100)
10. *"BACK ALLEY RIF"* (Malcolm Childers/Stephen Bigger, MIDI keyboards and samplers)--A fugue for nylon and steel strung guitar sounds........1:35
    Audio drama SUNDOWN ON THE DARK SIDE OF THE MOON (pages 102-4)
    Audio drama THE IDES OF GRATIFICATION (pages 106-108)
    Monologue FOR THE OCOEE AND OTHER SYLVAN DREAMS (pages 110-12)
11. *"PEACE RIVER/MAYBE WE'RE ALL JUST CHILDREN"* (Stephen Bigger, director; Chris Aymes, soloist; Rise' Gustafson, Kimolin Crutcher, Stephen and Susan Bigger, and LaFredrick Thirkill, singers)--A benediction for the future of humanity. Solo voice and then choral finale........2:35

END OF AUDIO CD TWO........Total time CD TWO........75:16

Recorded and produced at SunLion Music and Red Fish Records in Nashville, Tennessee, and The Real Earth Audioworks in Walden on Signal Mountain, Tennessee. Final mastering and production was done at Maple Ridge Studios, Landrum.com, in Ooltewah, Tennessee.

SHORT STORIES and POEMS for Readers

Book Printing Notes

A Review of the Technological Links Between the Etching Process and the Book

Back in 1965, Gene Franks, an older artist friend, and I would go into the countryside on drawing excursions. We would discuss reproducing our artwork, thinking that taking such risks would enable us to do good work and have a reasonable chance at financial compensation.

I realized that aspiration in the spring of 1968 when my father loaned me enough money to cover the cost of printing, and a friend donated some paper. I was in business. One of the 11 images from that printing is on page 156.

The best monochrome printing that I could arrange was 150-line duo-tone with one pass through the press in brown and one in black. While I was pleased with the 300 lines-per-inch resolution, something bothered me. In order for dense ink to create the illusion of a halftone, it has to be laid down in millions of fine discrete dots. Conventional halftone screens make dots in straight mechanical rows. These rows can add a subliminal mechanical feel to printed work. It was my desire to avoid that mechanical feel, which motivated me through much of the following journey:

1969- I took a graphic arts class at Riverside Community College. My father had some AB Dick and Addressagraph Multigraph direct print duplicator plates from his printing job. I drew on them with the special wax pencils that came with the plates, then I took the finished plates to class and printed my drawings on a small offset press. I got a few good impressions. These were my first tonal prints without mechanical screens.

1970-72 While taking various printmaking classes in college, I studied all the main printmaking methods and learned that etching and lithography were capable of yielding the kind of tonal range I wanted in an original print.

1973- I developed the relief etching process for the thirty etching images in this book. They had a tonal and textural range of embossed random ink dots wonderfully free of any mechanical screen.

1975-88 Gene Hill, a graphics cameraman at Jones Printing Company in Chattanooga, Tennessee, worked with me to make the line negatives for over half of the images in this book.

1982- With the entrepreneurial help of Bill Wager and Bill Anspach, two dentists from Reno, I engaged in a new high-tech printmaking process that began with hand-drawing color separations on frosted plastic sheets and ended by printing two consistent editions of ten-color images printed on a five-station, forty-inch Heidelberg press.

I called the process plano-transligraphy (planographic-light-drawing). From a print image standpoint, the results were magnificent. The images were perfectly screenless, continuous tone, and full color.

1994-97 My wife Pamela, Mark Caldwell and I decided to create this book. One problem was immediately apparent--the only cost-effective method of printing a book was halftone screen reproduction. Having gone through years of work to escape the screen, how would I now convey the unique value of tones from random dots if finally everything had to be filtered through the old conventional halftone screens?

Fortunately, I found a new computer-generated, random-dot process known as stochastic printing. Upon very close examination, the difference between stochastic and conventional halftone screen printing could be analogous to looking out of a sliding glass patio door. The stochastic version appears crisp, like looking through clean glass. The conventional half-tone appears like the patio door covered by the sliding screen. There tends to be less resolution and contrast.

1997 - 1999 After months of research, getting bids and proofs, ironically Jones Printing Company was selected to printing the text block of this book in four stochastic and one solid color.

Epilogue

MARVIN E. CHILDERS

Behind our eyes are the roads we have traveled. In our emotions are the songs we have sung. At the core of our very being is a lifeline, traceable backwards through all the years of our conscious memory--childhood, infancy, birth, and conception. But the line recedes behind us into the continuous adaptation of our ancestral DNA to the changes in environment that have evolved our cerebral cortex, our mammalian and reptilian brains, and our central nervous system. Finally, that line links us to the simple organisms that came from the same basic elements that make up this speck of living island called Earth and the unfathomable cosmic ocean through which we move.

Any deep connection that we long for, with each other and the cosmos that makes up our reality, will come from our continuing quest to prove, reprove and improve our knowledge of this living mystery. The more we know about our origins, the more we will be able to understand and prepare for the future. Nothing will prepare us better for this adventure than to remember and regain the fascination for life that we had when we were very young.

Index of ROADSONGS Relief Etchings

All Images Hand Pulled by Malcolm Graeme Childers

IMAGE/PAGE	IMAGE TITLE	EDITION SIZE	AVAILABILITY
13	AT A CROSSROADS ON STATE 38	260	available
17	SIERRA BEFORE THE STORM	260	available
21	NEVADA NORTHERN FREIGHT #81	50	edition exhausted
25	ONYX STORE	50	edition exhausted
29	THE SEMI	50	edition exhausted
35	FRENCHY'S FLATHEAD FLYER on the right day	260	available
39	ON THE CUTTING EDGE OF TEMPORARY	260	available
43	BACK TO NATURE	260	available
47	ASCENT FROM #3	260	available
51	AMID THE BEAMS AND RUST OF DAYS GONE BY, WE FIND MANY ANOTHER MAN'S SUNRISE	50	edition exhausted
55	WOODEN MASTODON	50	edition exhausted
59	DARWIN ARCO SERVICE	50	edition exhausted
63	HIGH BAROQUE FOR THE HEARTLAND	250	available
67	A FUNERAL FOR VENUS: So Much for Good Intentions	260	available
71	DESDICHADO: An Echo of Stolen Thunder	260	available
75	TALKIN' DURANGO FLUES	250	available
79	THE FLATCAR, BLANCA, COLORADO	50	edition exhausted
83	THE ROCK ISLAND LINE NEAR ITS VANISHING POINT	260	available
87	S.P. DIESEL #3665	50	edition exhausted
91	'53 BUICK ROADMASTER	50	edition exhausted
95	ORO GRANDE MARKET	50	edition exhausted
99	FIRST LESSONS IN CONVERSATIONAL TRUCK	260	available
103	SUNDOWN ON THE DARKSIDE OF THE MOON	250	available
107	THE IDES OF GRATIFICATION	250	available
111	FOR THE OCOEE and Other Sylvan Dreams	260	available
115	'48 PLYMOUTH	50	edition exhausted
123	SOME WITH STRONG BACKS WAINING	50	edition exhausted
131	A PROPHET IN OXIDE	50	edition exhausted
137	FRONT RANGE GOLD	260	available
141	LOCKHEED LODESTAR	50	edition exhausted

For further information visit the ROADSONGS website at www.roadsongs.com or call 1-888-488-6714.